Book 7L

Cast your eyes to the ocean
Cast your soul to the sea
When the dark night seems endless
Please remember me

Loreena McKennitt from Dante's Prayer

Contact the author:

autor@claudia-edelmann.de
www.claudia-edelmann.de

*A share per sold copy of this book will be given
to support the Kōhanga Reo Schools in Aotearoa.*

*Vom Erlös dieses Buches geht pro verkauftem Exemplar
ein Anteil an die Kōhanga Reo-Schulen in Neuseeland.*

1. Auflage September 2011
Copyright: Wolfram Kühnert Verlag
Layout Umschlag: Claudia Edelmann
Layout und Gestaltung Buchblock: Wolfram Kühnert
Bild Seite 4: Daniel Ormsby
Cheflektor Englisch und Māori: Piripi Waretini
Druck: Druckerei Uhl, Radolfzell
ISBN 978-3-9813220-1-9

1. Edition September 2011
Copyright: Wolfram Kühnert Verlag
Layout book cover: Claudia Edelmann
Painting page 4: Daniel Ormsby
Chief Editor English and Māori: Piripi Waretini
Print: Uhl, Radolfzell, Germany
ISBN 978-3-9813220-1-9

Claudia Edelmann

Māori

Neuseelands verborgener Schatz

Ngā Taonga i te Huna
o Aotearoa

New Zealand's Hidden Treasure

Wolfram Kühnert
Verlag für Belletristik & Reiseliteratur

Dedicated to
Sonny (Baldy) Otimi
with love

Inhalt – Ngā Whakaritenga – Content

This is a humble supplication to the omniscient creator
Whose sacred spirit is imbued upon this new book
To be widely distributed, regarded and retained throughout the world
Spiritually enlivened with vitality
And supported by the essence of all peoples
Under the guidance provided by the creator
'As you are omnipotent
Powerful and glorious, throughout eternity'
Let peace reside.

Foreword

Kia ora,

The last year was significant, eventful and very exciting for me. It was a year that I mainly spent in New Zealand Aotearoa, in order to do the research for this book.

From the beginning the work has filled me with deep joy and gratitude as I experienced the people who are the main subject on the following pages, the Māori.

It is a great privilege for me that the Māori people allowed me to get a deep insight into their culture. I am very happy about the deep connection that has developed between me and the Māori. Not only that they became friends, but that they also became *whānau*, extended family.

The support that I have experienced while I was working on this book was overwhelming and I dearly miss my friends in Aotearoa.

Dear reader, while you are exploring this book I hope that I am able to put the same intense feeling of happiness into your hearts like the one I experienced while I was working on completing this book.

Tēnā koutou, tēnā koutou, tēnā koutou katoa.

Aroha nui and kind regards

C. Ed

Ko tēnei he koropiko ki te atua kaha rawa
e ūwhia nei nā tōna wairua tapu ki runga ki tēnei pukapuka hou
kia tūwhera atu ki te rongo nui me te rongo mau ki ngā pitopito o te ao.
Whakaurua mai te mauri ora, te hīhiri nui o te wairua
ki ngā ira tāngata hei āwhina mai i te kaupapa nei.
Hei ārahi atu e te Atua.
Nō reira ko koe, te rangatiratanga
te kaha me te korōria, ake tonu atu
Pai marie.

Vorwort

Kia ora,

das letzte Jahr war für mich bedeutungsvoll, ereignisreich und aufregend zugleich. Es war ein Jahr, das ich hauptsächlich in Neuseeland verbrachte, um dort die Recherchen zu vorliegendem Buch zu unternehmen.

Die Arbeit an diesem Projekt hat mich von Anfang an mit tiefer Freude und Dankbarkeit erfüllt, da ich es mit den Menschen realisieren konnte, die auf den nachfolgenden Seiten im Mittelpunkt stehen: die Māori.

Die Unterstützung, die ich bei diesem Buchprojekt von Seiten der Māori erfahren habe ist überwältigend, und es freut mich sagen zu können, dass ich nicht ein Buch *über* die Māori, sondern *mit* den Māori geschrieben habe.

Es ist ein großes Vorrecht für mich, dass mich die Māori bei sich aufgenommen haben und ich in all der Zeit ihr Gast sein durfte. Ich habe diese Menschen aufrichtig lieben und schätzen gelernt und ich bin glücklich, dass sie enge Freunde und Familie für mich geworden sind.

Liebe Leserin, lieber Leser, ich wünsche mir, dass es mir auf den nachfolgenden Seiten gelingt, in Ihre Herzen das intensive Gefühl des Glücks zu legen, das ich während der Arbeit an diesem Buch verspürte.

Tēnā koutou, tēnā koutou, tēnā koutou katoa.

Herzlichst Ihre

C. Ed

Unterwegs im King Country

Als Basis für meine Recherchen in Neuseeland diente der kleine Ort Te Kuiti im King Country in der Waikato-Region. Der Name Te Kuiti leitet sich von dem Wort „*Te Kuititanga*" ab, was als „Tal der Verengung" wiedergegeben werden kann. Einer der kulturellen Anziehungspunkte des Städtchens ist das Versammlungshaus Te Tōkanganui-a-Noho, das dem lokalen Māori-Stamm Ngāti Maniapoto als zentrale Anlaufstelle dient.

Als ich in die Kultur der Māori eintauchte wusste ich nicht, was mich erwarten würde. Um dieses Buch schreiben zu können, war ich darauf angewiesen, dass sich die Māori mir gegenüber öffneten und mir vertrauten. Doch sie taten mehr als das, sie erlaubten mir ein Teil von ihnen zu werden.

Nachfolgend möchte ich Ihnen die Personen vorstellen mit denen ich mich ganz besonders verbunden fühle, und die einen besonderen Anteil am Gelingen dieses Buches haben.

On the Road in the King Country

My research in New Zealand was based in the small town of Te Kuiti in the King Country in the Waikato region. The name Te Kuiti derives from the word "*Te Kuititanga*", which can be translated as "The narrowing". A key cultural attraction of the place is the wonderfully carved meeting house Te Tōkanganui - a - Noho that serves as central point of contact to the local tribe Ngāti Maniapoto.

As I entered the indigenous culture of Māori, I did not know what to expect. To be able to write this book I had to depend on the willingness of Māori to open up and trust me. They actually did more than that because they endowed me with the privilege to become a part of them.

Now I would like to introduce you to a people who are very precious to me, a people who have a special role and part in the completion of this book.

Nordinsel

(Map labels: Cape Reinga, Auckland, Hamilton, Rotorua, Te Kuiti, Taupo, Wellington)

Countryside close to Mokau, North Island
Landschaft in der Nähe von Mokau, Nordinsel

Tokowhā aus Te Kuiti

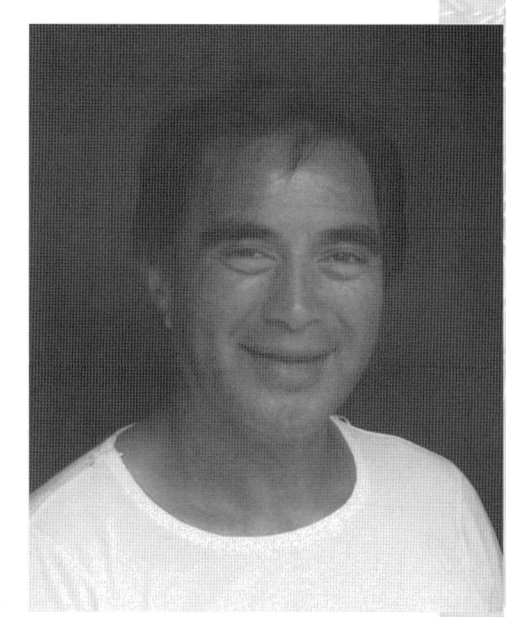

Obwohl ich bereits 1992 zum ersten Mal nach Neuseeland reiste, war im Jahr 2008 Tokowhā der erste Māori mit dem ich in persönlichen Kontakt kam. Dieser Mann war ein hervorragender Lehrer und Türöffner für mich, und während meines Aufenthalts in Neuseeland stellte er mir als Gastgeber in seinem Haus in Te Kuiti großzügig ein Zimmer und ein Fahrzeug zur Verfügung. Tokowhā hat mir gleich zu Beginn meiner Recherchearbeit einen Rat gegeben: „Wenn du mein Volk wirklich kennenlernen und verstehen möchtest, dann musst du mit ihnen essen, mit ihnen trinken, mit ihnen lachen, mit ihnen weinen, mit ihnen arbeiten und mit ihnen ausruhen."

Ich habe mir Tokowhās Empfehlungen zu Herzen genommen und bei all diesen Gelegenheiten Menschen kennengelernt, deren Wertvorstellungen, deren enge Familienbande und deren Respekt vor der Natur mich tief beeindruckt haben. Wenn Sie mich fragen, wie ich meinen Gastgeber Tokowhā beschreiben würde, dann müsste ich ihn wohl mit einem kleinen Tornado vergleichen. Dieser Mann war zumeist der perfekte Begleiter, wenn seine Methoden auch nicht immer die sensibelsten waren. Stets erwies er sich als sehr ungeduldig, noch einmal nachzufragen wenn man etwas nicht verstanden hatte zeitigte tiefe Sorgenfalten auf seiner Stirn. Er war immer leidenschaftlich in seinen Empfehlungen und oftmals gelangte man zu der Einsicht, dass nur seine Meinung die einzig wahre ist.

Was meine schriftstellerische Arbeit anging, hatte Tokowhā eine klare Vorstellung davon, wie ich diese durchzuführen hatte. Nicht nur einmal hat er mir an den Kopf geworfen, dass ich ein unfähiger Journalist sei, weil er mit meiner ständigen Planung und meiner Arbeitsweise, die ein mehrfaches Interviewen derselben Person zur Folge hatte, nicht konform ging. Er war sehr hitzig und erlaubte sich eine Meinung, wo ihm meiner Ansicht nach überhaupt keine zustand.

Zudem war ihm das Wort „Manieren" unbekannt und wer Knigge war hat sich ihm wohl bis heute nicht erschlossen. War ich es gewohnt, dass mir ein Kavalier mit meinem Gepäck half, so saß mein Gastgeber seelenruhig im Auto und beobachtete durch den Rückspiegel, wie ich mich mit meinem Koffer abmühte. „You packed it, you carry it" waren seine Worte, aus denen ich oftmals am liebsten einen Strick gedreht und ihn damit erwürgt hätte.

Oft tobte Tokowhā mit Donnerstimme über meinen Kopf hinweg, und von einer Sekunde auf die andere fiel seine Stimmung von „sonnig" auf „Gewitter inklusive Hagelschlag". Zumeist gelang es mir nicht, die Ursache der schlechten „Wetterlage" herauszufinden, und als Resultat dessen fand ich mich häufig fluchend auf dem nahegelegenen Sportplatz wieder. Dort drehte ich solange meine Runden, bis ich meinen inneren Frieden wieder gefunden hatte und mich in der Lage sah, ins Haus zurückzukehren.

Was auch immer die Beweggründe für sein Verhalten waren, jedem Schreibenden unter Ihnen ist klar, dass solche erschwerten Bedingungen einen bedeutenden Einfluss auf die empfindliche Schreiberseele haben können. Vor allem in den entscheidenden Phasen seiner Arbeit, bei denen es ums Formulieren und Ausarbeiten geht, sehnt sich ein Autor nach Ruhe und Ausgeglichenheit.

Doch mein Gastgeber hat auch gute Seiten. Wenn er anfängt zu lehren, dann saugt man begierig jeden einzelnen Buchstaben in sich auf. Er ist ein Meister der Worte, die er harmonisch aneinanderreiht wie die Perlen einer kostbaren Halskette, und jedes einzelne von ihnen spielt er wie eine gut gestimmte Violine. Worte, die lieblich, aber auch verletzend sein können, so manch unschöner Begriff ziert seine Reden, doch die Botschaft ist stets von hohem Wert.

Ungern sah es mein Gastgeber wenn ich, kaum dass er zu reden anfing, mein Aufnahmegerät zückte. Als ich ihn wieder einmal darum bat seine Rede aufzeichnen zu dürfen, hat er mir die Geschichte seines Urgroßvaters (*koro*) erzählt, der ihn als Kind dazu einlud an einer Versammlung teilzunehmen. Tokowhā wollte ins Haus zurück um dort Stift und Papier zu holen, aber sein Urgroßvater sagte: „Wenn du Stift und Papier brauchst um dich an das Gesagte zu erinnern, dann bleib' zuhause." Als Kind hat Tokowhā nicht verstanden was sein Urgroßvater ihm damit sagen wollte, erst später in seinem Leben wurde ihm die Botschaft klar, die er mir wie folgt erklärte: Lerne mit deinem Herzen zu hören, dann brauchst du weder Stift noch Papier.

Wie turbulent die Zeit in Tokowhās Haus auch für mich gewesen ist, am Ende bleibt mir nur eines zu sagen: Ohne meinen Gastgeber Tokowhā wäre dieses Buch niemals zustande gekommen und dafür werde ich ihm immer dankbar und tief verbunden sein.

June James aus Te Kuiti

Gleich bei meinem ersten Besuch in Te Kuiti hat Tokowhā einen Kontakt zwischen mir und der charmanten June hergestellt. Innerhalb kürzester Zeit wurde June zu einer engen Freundin und Vertrauten. Während meines Aufenthalts in Te Kuiti verging kaum ein Tag, an dem wir keinen Kontakt hatten.

Pipiana Hetet aus Papamoa

„Ich habe leider nichts zu erzählen", erklärte Pipiana bei unserer ersten Begegnung, doch im Gegensatz zu ihr war ich mir sicher, dass sie voller Geschichten steckte. Pipiana und ich mochten uns auf Anhieb und obwohl sie schon kurz nach unserem ersten Gespräch nach Papamoa an die Ostküste zog, war ich häufiger Gast in ihrem Haus. Unsere gemeinsame Leidenschaft waren Miso-Suppe und Guacamole, Speisen, die ich jedes Mal zubereitete, wenn ich sie besuchte.

Daniel Ormsby aus Waitomo

Der junge Māori-Künstler Daniel war mir besonders bei dem Thema „Tā Moko", der traditionellen Māori Tätowierung, eine große Hilfe. Geduldig beantwortete er meine Fragen und versorgte mich überdies mit ausreichend Informationsmaterial zu verschiedenen anderen Themen, die Teil meiner Recherche waren.

Angela & Piripi Waretini aus Christchurch

Bereits in Neuseeland beschäftigte mich die Frage, wen ich mit der Übersetzung einiger Geschichten in die Māori-Sprache bemühen sollte. Kurz darauf traf ich Angela und Piripi, die für diese Aufgabe gerade prädestiniert waren. Selbst nach meiner Rückkehr nach Deutschland und einer Distanz von 20 000 Kilometern standen mir die beiden mit Rat und Tat zur Seite.

Pipiana Hetet, now living in Papamoa

"Unfortunately I don't have anything to tell", Pipiana said on our first encounter, despite what she said I was sure that she was full of interesting stories. Pipiana and I liked each other right away. She moved to Papamoa on the East Coast shortly after our first meeting and I became a frequent guest in her home. Miso soup and guacamole was our favourite shared passion at each visit.

Daniel Ormsby from Waitomo

The young Māori artist Daniel helped me a lot while I was doing the research on *"Tā moko"*, the traditional Māori tattooing. Patiently Daniel answered all my questions and also provided me with a lot of information on various issues that were part of my research.

Angela & Piripi Waretini from Christchurch

Already in New Zealand, I wondered who I could ask to do the translation of some English written stories into the Māori language. Shortly afterwards, I met Angela and Piripi who were perfectly qualified for this task. Even after my return to Germany and at a distance of 20 000 kilometres, they gave me advice and support.

June James from Te Kuiti

I met June during my first visit in Te Kuiti when my host Tokowhā introduced me to this charming lady. Within a short time June became like a sister and close friend to me and hardly a day went by where we had no contact.

Tokowhā from Te Kuiti

Although I first travelled to New Zealand in the early 1990s I never had a personal contact with a Māori until I met Tokowhā in 2008. This man has been a great teacher and door opener for me and at the very beginning he gave me some advice. Tokowhā said: If you want to meet and fully understand my people, then you have to eat with them, drink with them, laugh with them, cry with them, work with them and rest with them. That's what I have done and on all these occasions I have met people whose values, close family ties and respect for nature have deeply impressed me.

During my stay in New Zealand Tokowhā took on the role as my host and also provided me with a room and a car. If you ask me how I would describe Tokowhā, I would most likely compare him to a tornado. In most cases this man was the perfect supporter even if his methods were not always the most sensitive. He was often very impatient and if I did not understand something quickly, deep worry lines developed on his forehead stopping me from asking for further clarification.

He was always passionate in his

recommendations and I often came to the conclusion that his opinion was "the true one". More than once he told me that I was an incapable journalist because he could not accept my constant planning and the way I did my job, which often included interviewing the same person several times.

He was very fiery, provided with a strong dash of anger and expressed his opinion in situations where I felt he absolutely had no right. Besides that the word "manners" didn't exist at all in his vocabulary and even now the meaning of the expression "good behaviour" has not yet opened up to him. In Germany I was used to some friendly person offering to help me with my luggage but in New Zealand my host sat calmly in this car watching through the mirror while I struggled with my suitcase. "You packed it, you carry it," were his words I often was tempted to turn a rope and strangle him with it.

Tokowhā often went wild, his thunderous voice rolling over my head and from one moment to the other his mood went from "sunny" to "hailstorm". In most cases I didn't manage to work out the cause of the poor "weather conditions" and as a result I often found myself at the nearby sports ground swearing and running in circles until I regained my inner peace and composure once again.

Whatever the motives for his actions, every writer knows that such extreme conditions have a significant impact on the sensitive writer's soul, and in the crucial stages of his work an author yearns for peace and harmony.

It needs to be said that Tokowhā also has good qualities. When he begins to teach you can't help but become eagerly absorbed by every word. He is a master of words which he strings together in complete harmony like the pearls of a precious necklace and every single word he plays like a well-tuned violin. Words, loving but also painful and many aggressive expressions decorate his speeches, but the lesson is always one of great value.

When he began to share and I dared to pull out my tape recorder he reacted with obvious reluctance. Many times I tried to outsmart him as I ran my recorder secretly under the table or just hidden in the palm of my hand. In most cases the quality of the recorded speeches was so bad that I could not use them and I couldn't do anything other than simply feel pity for the loss of the precious words.

No matter how turbulent the times I spent in Tokowhā's house have been the truth is that without him this book would not have been possible and therefore I will always love and respect him.

Left side: 90 Mile Beach, North Island

Next page: A look into New Zealand's rain forest, North Island
Nächste Seite: Ein Blick in Neuseelands Regenwald, Nordinsel

ॐ 15 ॐ

Eine alte Liebe – Neuseeland und ich

He ngau aroha, ko Aotearoa,

ko au, ko au, ko Aotearoa

A Precious Love – New Zealand and I

He tini ngā whetū e ngaro i te kapua iti
Many stars can be concealed by a small cloud

Sehnsucht ist unheilbar

Geschichten haben oftmals seltsame Anfänge, und diese begann mit der Suche nach einem Alibi - einem Alibi, das mir einen mehrmonatigen Aufenthalt in Neuseeland ermöglichen würde. Meine bisherigen Besuche dort waren Urlaube gewesen, in denen ich das Land erkundet und die weitläufigen Strände genossen hatte. Als ich zu Beginn der 1990er Jahre zum ersten Mal in Auckland auf der Nordinsel ankam, schlich sich Neuseeland sofort in mein Herz und setzte dort seinen Anker.

Doch was war mit den *Māori**, der indigenen Bevölkerung Neuseelands? Zum damaligen Zeitpunkt wusste ich nur das über sie, was man in jedem Reiseführer lesen konnte. Ehrlich gesagt war ich auch nicht über die Maßen an ihrer Geschichte und ihrem Schicksal interessiert. Mich faszinierte die Landschaft Neuseelands, die schneebedeckten Berge, die undurchdringlichen Regenwälder, die rauschenden Wasserfälle, die Stille und Einsamkeit, die sofort verfügbar war, wenn ich mich danach sehnte.

Irgendwann im Laufe meiner Reise habe ich die Waitangi Treaty Grounds in Paihia besucht, einen historischen Ort, an dem es im Jahr 1840 zum Treaty of Waitangi gekommen ist, einer Vereinbarung, die sowohl den Māori als auch den eingewanderten Siedlern ein friedliches Zusammenleben in *Aotearoa* (der Name der Māori für Neuseeland) garantieren sollte. Jahrelange brutale Kriege, die auf beiden Seiten einen hohen Blutzoll gefordert hatten, waren dem Friedensvertrag vorausgegangen. Die Briten waren in das Gebiet eingefallen, fest entschlossen sich zu nehmen was sie wollten, das Land der Māori. Wer nicht kooperierte und die begehrten Landflächen freiwillig herausgab, der wurde kurzerhand enteignet oder mit Waffengewalt überzeugt. Leider erfüllten sich die Hoffnungen, die man in den Treaty of Waitangi gesetzt hatte, zunächst nicht und die Kämpfe zwischen den Europäern und den Māori dauerten noch viele Jahre an. Auf dem Gelände der Waitangi Treaty Grounds erinnert heute ein dreißig Meter langes Kriegskanu (*waka taua*) sowie ein reich mit Schnitzereien verziertes Versammlungshaus (*whare hui*) an die Māori-Kultur. Wer glaubt, dass ich während meines Aufenthalts auf dem Areal unzähligen Māori begegnet bin der irrt, ich traf keinen einzigen.

Informationen über die Māori bezog ich aus Tageszeitungen, in denen regelmäßig über die von ihnen begangenen Straftaten berichtet wurde. Die Arbeitslosenquote war hoch und nur wenige erlangten einen ausreichenden Schulabschluss. Unterhielt ich mich mit den ansässigen Europäern (*Pākehā*), so musste ich feststellen, dass diese nicht gerade mit überschwänglicher Begeisterung

* alle Begriffe aus der Sprache Māori sind im Glossar erklärt

von ihren indigenen Nachbarn sprachen. Es war von Disputen die Rede, in denen es um Land- und Besitzrechte ging.

Die Europäer beklagten die mangelnde Bereitschaft der Māori sich an ihre Kultur anzupassen und die Weigerung die damit verbundenen Vorteile zu sehen.

Während meiner Reise durch Neuseeland schienen sich die Berichterstattung der Presse und die Einschätzung der europäischen Anwohner nur zu oft zu bestätigen. Passierte ich Māori-Siedlungen, sah es dort zumeist unordentlich und ungepflegt aus. Übergewichtige Menschen saßen auf ihren Terrassen oder lungerten auf der Straße herum, rauchten und tranken Bier. Manche trugen Tätowierungen, entweder im Gesicht oder großflächig auf ihren Körpern verteilt. Die Häuser waren verwahrlost, die Gärten verwildert. Ich gewann den Eindruck, dass körperliche Arbeit nicht gerade zu den favorisierten Betätigungen der Māori gehörte. Die meisten Familien schienen reichlich mit Kindern gesegnet zu sein und anstatt selbst für den Lebensunterhalt zu sorgen, vertrauten sie wohl in erster Linie auf die Unterstützung des Staates, die in Form der Sozialhilfe einmal in der Woche pünktlich auf dem Konto einging. Dazu kamen Berichte von gewaltbereiten Gangs, die die Straßen unsicher machten und in der Bevölkerung für Angst und Schrecken sorgten. All das warf kein gutes Bild auf die Māori und nach dem was ich gesehen und gehört hatte verspürte ich keinerlei Verlangen, mit ihnen in Kontakt zu treten.

Ich muss zugeben ich war voller Vorurteile, Vorurteile gegenüber Menschen, von denen ich keinen einzigen persönlich kannte. Bestenfalls hatte ich einmal mit einem Māori im ´Fish and Chips-Laden´ gemeinsam auf eine Bestellung gewartet und das ohne ein einziges Wort mit ihm zu wechseln. Meine Begeisterung galt dem Land, das mir Tag für Tag eine neue Dosis seines süßen Gifts injizierte. Ich wollte immer mehr davon haben und als ich nach fünf Wochen die Heimreise antrat war ich eine Abhängige, ständig von der Idee besessen so bald wie möglich nach Aotearoa zurückzukehren. Innerhalb der nächsten Jahre flog ich noch siebenmal nach Neuseeland, zu einem persönlichen Kontakt mit den Māori kam es dabei nie.

*

Jetzt, fast zwanzig Jahre nach meinem ersten Besuch in Neuseeland hatte sich die Idee in meinem Kopf eingenistet die Māori kennenzulernen und über sie zu schreiben. Zweifellos drängt sich die Frage auf, was zu diesem Sinneswandel führte.

Lassen Sie es mich so erklären: Aotearoa hat mich niemals losgelassen und jede Rückreise, die in logischer Konsequenz auf jede Hinreise folgte, bereitete mir wahre Pein. Wenn mich das Flugzeug nach fast dreißigstündiger Reisezeit an einem deutschen Flughafen ausspuckte, fühlte ich mich innerlich wie ausgeraubt. Während ich den Koffer vom Gepäckband zog, war mein Herz noch immer in Neuseeland und machte keinerlei Anstalten, sich hier in Deutschland mit mir zu vereinen. In den normalen Alltag zurückzukehren fiel mir unendlich schwer und nahm mehrere Wochen in Anspruch.

Irgendwann hatte ich diesen unbefriedigenden Zustand satt und als sich vor ein paar Jahren die Möglichkeit bot meine berufliche Situation zu verändern, griff ich zu. Als Journalistin hatte ich viel mehr Spielraum, war örtlich nicht mehr gebunden und dadurch viel flexibler auch längere Reisen zu unternehmen. Neuseeland kam wieder in greifbare Nähe, doch mit ein paar Wochen wollte ich mich dieses Mal nicht zufriedengeben. Mehrere Monate ohne Ziel und Plan durch das Land zu reisen war dennoch nicht ohne weiteres möglich, es sei denn, etwas machte meine Anwesenheit dort erforderlich.

Und da war sie wieder: Die Suche nach dem Alibi. Doch mich mehrere Monate hinter einem mageren Alibi zu verstecken war nicht meine Art, ich brauchte eine Aufgabe, einen Auftrag. Ein Buchprojekt, das eine längere Zeit der Recherche notwendig machte, schien der perfekte Plan. Je länger ich mich mit dieser Idee auseinandersetzte, umso mehr gefiel sie mir. Doch worüber sollte ich schreiben? Zu viel war bereits über die Geschichte Neuseelands, seine Eroberung durch die Briten und die Kämpfe gegen die Māori aufgezeichnet worden.

Wenn ich über meine Einstellung zu den Māori nachdachte kam ich zu dem Schluss, dass ich ihnen eine neutrale und unvoreingenommene Haltung schuldete. Meine Einschätzung dieser Menschen beruhte ausschließlich auf dem, was ich gehört, gelesen und gesehen hatte. Nichts davon hatte ich in einem persönlichen Gespräch verifiziert. Ich hatte mich stets auf das Land konzentriert und dabei seine Menschen vergessen. Doch wie konnte ich behaupten ein Land zu kennen, wenn ich keinen einzigen seiner indigenen Bewohner kannte? Wie konnte ich behaupten ein Land zu lieben, wenn ich seine indigenen Bewohner nicht liebte? Doch bevor ich diese Menschen lieben konnte, musste ich sie kennenlernen. Eines war ohne das andere nicht möglich.

Doch war ich überhaupt qualifiziert genug, ein Buchprojekt wie dieses in Angriff zu nehmen, ausreichend befähigt über eine Kultur zu schreiben, über die ich nichts wusste? Bevor ich mit weiteren Planungen begann, beschloss ich meine Beweggründe und Qualifikationen zu überprüfen.

Ich bescheinige mir selbst einen klaren Verstand, den Willen mich auf Menschen einzulassen, sowie die Bereitschaft mein Herz mit Eindrücken zu füllen und aus diesem Überfluss heraus zu schreiben. Ich will immer alles ganz genau wissen und mit meiner ewigen Fragerei und der Suche nach Antworten kann ich meinen Mitmenschen ganz schön auf die Nerven gehen. Journalistin ist für mich der perfekte Beruf, auf legitime Art meinen Wissensdurst zu befriedigen. Die Suche nach der Wahrheit, nach Hintergründen, ist das, was mich an der Tätigkeit des Journalisten fasziniert. Dass bei der Berichterstattung die Wahrheit nicht immer an erster Stelle steht, das hatte ich in der

Vergangenheit erst lernen müssen. Manche Journalisten hatten sich dazu verleiten lassen das zu schreiben, was ihre Gesprächspartner wünschten.

Würde ich es ihnen in diesem Buch gleichtun? Die Antwort auf diese Frage hing wohl von der Motivation ab. Würde ich versuchen jemandem zu gefallen oder ging es mir einzig und allein um die unvoreingenommene Suche nach der Wahrheit? Die Suche nach der Wahrheit würde auch mal wehtun, sie war keine schmerzlose Angelegenheit. Bei dieser Recherche würden viele Emotionen im Spiel sein, was automatisch zu schmerzlichen Erinnerungen führen oder sogar lang aufgestauten Groll an die Oberfläche spülen würde. Wie würden die Māori mich als Gesprächspartner beurteilen? Wie würden ihnen meine Fragen gefallen? Würden sie mich in dieselbe Schublade stecken in der sich schon die Pākehā befanden, die sie um ihr Land gebracht und die ihre Vorfahren ermordet hatten?

Selbst wenn ich mir dieses Projekt zutraute, so musste ich zunächst einen Kontakt zu den Māori herstellen. Realistisch gesehen war ich etwa 20 000 Kilometer vom nächsten Māori entfernt - keine gute Ausgangssituation. Mir blieb also nur die Möglichkeit über das Internet mit einer Māori-Organisation in Verbindung zu treten.

Ich wandte mich zunächst an die Stelle, wo ich 1992 meinen ersten verhaltenen Kontakt mit der Māori-Kultur gehabt hatte, an den Waitangi National Trust in Paihia. Nach mehreren Wochen teilte man mir per E-Mail mit, dass man nach genauer Betrachtung zu der Entscheidung gekommen war, mich weder bei meinem Vorhaben unterstützen noch mir bei der Kontaktaufnahme zu Māori-Familien helfen zu können. Eine andere Organisation, die ich zeitgleich angeschrieben hatte, blieb mir bis heute die Antwort schuldig. Enttäuscht durchsuchte ich das Internet nach weiteren Kontaktquellen, allerdings ohne Erfolg. Es sah so aus als würde mein Projekt scheitern, bevor es überhaupt begonnen hatte.

Doch kurz darauf kam mir das Schicksal in Form eines Veranstaltungshinweises zu Hilfe. Ein Māori wollte an meinem Wohnort in einer Foto-Show über Neuseeland berichten. Ungläubig starrte ich auf die kleine Notiz, die mir das verhieß was ich suchte, einen Māori.

Eine erste Begegnung

Zahlreich waren die Menschen an diesem Abend der Einladung gefolgt, die unter dem Motto „Neuseeland - das Land der Māori" stand. Ich wusste, dass es nicht gut für mich sein würde Bilder von Neuseeland zu sehen, da sich dadurch sofort das dringende Bedürfnis bei mir einstellen würde, mit gepackten Koffern zum nächstgelegenen Flughafen zu fahren. Mein Plan war es daher, noch vor Beginn der Veranstaltung den Kontakt zu dem Māori herzustellen und danach so schnell wie möglich wieder zu verschwinden. Doch die Bühne war leer, von dem Māori keine Spur. Es blieb mir nichts anderes übrig als mir einen Platz zu suchen und zu warten. Nach etwa zehn Minuten betrat ein in Jeans und Pullover gekleideter Mann den Raum. „Mein Name ist Tokowhā und ich komme aus Neuseeland", sagte er in gebrochenem Deutsch. Kurz darauf zog Neuseelands Landschaft an mir vorüber und obwohl ich mich dagegen wehrte, nahm mich die Stimmung innerhalb von Sekunden gefangen und riss mich mit sich fort.

Als die Foto-Show zu Ende war nahm Tokowhā die Anwesenden mit auf eine Reise in seine Kindheit in die 1950er Jahre. Er erzählte davon, wie er von seinem Lehrer, einem Pākehā, seines Vornamens beraubt worden war. Da sein Lehrer „Tokowhā" in der Aussprache als zu schwierig befand, gab er ihm kurzerhand den Vornamen „John". Auf die Narbe deutend, die auf seiner Stirn zu sehen war, berichtete Tokowhā davon, wie er in der Schule misshandelt worden war, weil er Māori statt Englisch gesprochen hatte. Unterstützung hatte er in diesen schwierigen Zeiten von seinem Urgroßvater erhalten, der ihn immer wieder ermuntert hatte, stolz auf seine Māori-Wurzeln zu sein. Das Schicksal dieses kleinen Jungen, der all das über sich ergehen lassen musste, weil er der „falschen" Rasse entstammte und die „falsche" Hautfarbe hatte, berührte mich tief.

Als es eine Pause gab, war ich regelrecht erleichtert und bevor mir jemand zuvorkommen konnte, stürmte ich geradewegs auf den Māori zu. Ohne große Vorrede überfiel ich ihn mit den Worten: „Mein Name ist Claudia, ich bin Journalistin und möchte gerne über dein Volk schreiben." Der Māori blieb zunächst stumm und sah mich mit seinen schwarzen Augen durchdringend an, so als versuche er, sich ein Bild von mir zu machen. Dann sagte er: „Komm in mein Haus nach Neuseeland und schreibe über mein Volk."

Noch bevor der zweite Teil der Veranstaltung begann, verließ ich mit einer Visitenkarte in der Hand den Saal. Ich konnte kaum glauben, was sich in den letzten Minuten ereignet hatte. Die Begegnung mit Tokowhā würde mir die Möglichkeit eröffnen nach Neuseeland zu reisen und meine Buchidee zu realisieren. Ich wusste zwar noch nicht wann ich diese Reise antreten würde, doch ich würde Himmel und Erde in Bewegung setzen, dass es bald sein würde.

Am nächsten Abend schrieb ich Tokowhā eine E-Mail, in der ich mich für sein Angebot bedankte, mir bei dem Buchprojekt zu helfen. Er hielt sich noch einige Wochen in Deutschland auf und gerne hätte ich in einem Gespräch noch mehr Einblick in das Schicksal der Māori erhalten. Tokowhā wollte versuchen ein Treffen mit mir zu arrangieren, doch ohne ihn noch einmal zu Gesicht zu bekommen, flog er kurze Zeit später nach Neuseeland zurück.

At Cape Reinga on my first visit to New Zealand in 1992
Am Cape Reinga während meines ersten Besuchs in Neuseeland im Jahr 1992

On the South Island in 1992
Auf der Südinsel im Jahr 1992

The cradle of Bungy-Jumping: Kawarau Bridge close to Queenstown in 1992
Die Wiege des Bungy-Jumping: Die Kawarau Brücke bei Queenstown,1992

My mother arriving in Auckland in 1994
Die Ankunft meiner Mutter in Neuseeland im Jahr 1994

Right page: Tongariro National Park, North Island

Ich hütete Tokowhās Visitenkarte wie meinen Augapfel. Ein ganzes Jahr verging, in dem ich mich bemühte den Kontakt mit ihm per E-Mail aufrecht zu erhalten. Tokowhā schrieb nicht oft und wenn er schrieb, dann nicht viel, doch ich war zufrieden, wenn er überhaupt antwortete, wenn auch nur aus Höflichkeit. So übertrieben es auch klingen mag, aber ich war auf diesen Mann angewiesen, ohne ihn war die Realisierung dieses Buches nicht möglich.

Als es Sommer wurde, informierte mich Tokowhā per E-Mail darüber, dass er bald in Deutschland eintreffen würde. Da es Zeit war meine Reisepläne zu konkretisieren, war ich sehr daran interessiert ihn zu treffen. Ein paar Tage später stand er plötzlich vor meiner Haustür. Ich weiß nicht mehr, was er mir an diesem Abend alles erzählte, ich weiß nur, dass es viel war, zu viel für einen Menschen, den man gar nicht kennt. Er redete leise, fast tonlos und ab und zu, wenn die Finsternis der Vergangenheit ihren Schatten über ihn legte, wurde sein Gesicht von Schmerz umspült. Als Tokowhā Stunden später ging, saß ich erst noch eine Weile in völliger Stille, um seine Worte auf mich wirken zu lassen.

Tokowhā hatte meine Neugierde geweckt und für einen der folgenden Abende lud ich ihn zum Essen ein. Doch obwohl er sein Kommen zugesagt hatte, erschien er nicht, kein Anruf, keine Mitteilung. Gehörte diese Unzuverlässigkeit zur Kultur der Māori? War sie ein Vorgeschmack dessen, was mich in Neuseeland erwarten würde?

Tokowhā kam einen Tag später, die verpasste Einladung erwähnte er nicht. Als ich ihn darauf ansprach meinte er nur: „Ich esse abends sowieso nicht", damit war das Thema vom Tisch. In den nächsten Stunden entführte er mich erneut in seine Vergangenheit.

Diese weitere Begegnung mit Tokowhā bestärkte mich in dem Entschluss, so bald wie möglich nach Neuseeland zu reisen. Obwohl ich noch immer keine Informationen darüber hatte, wie sich mein Aufenthalt in Tokowhās Haus gestalten würde, durchsuchte ich noch an diesem Abend das Internet nach einem passenden Flug. Ohne lange zu überlegen legte ich meine Abreise auf Mitte Januar fest.

Bereits drei Monate vor der geplanten Reise begann ich mit dem Kofferpacken, ein deutliches Indiz dafür, dass ich den Abflug kaum erwarten konnte. Um mein dürftiges Wissen über die Kultur der Māori aufzubessern beschaffte ich mir Bücher, die ich begierig verschlang. Doch das was ich las reichte nicht im Geringsten aus, um mir ein klares Bild von diesen Menschen zu machen. Es blieb mir nichts anderes übrig, als meine Neugier in Zaum zu halten und geduldig auf den Tag meiner Abreise zu warten.

Endlich Neuseeland

Der Regenwald war ein magischer Ort, ich liebte es ihn zu durchstreifen. Der Himmel war durch das dichte Blättergeflecht kaum sichtbar, die Zikaden stimmten ihr Lied an und die Vögel, die in den Baumkronen im Wind schaukelten, tschilpten vergnügt. Es schien fast so, als wollten sie mich antreiben, nun endlich meine Reise in die mir noch unbekannte Welt der Māori zu beginnen.

Mehrere Tage war ich nun bereits in Neuseeland. Meine Mutter, die vor vielen Jahren ebenfalls ihr Herz an dieses Land verloren hatte, begleitete mich für drei Wochen. Meinem Buchprojekt stand sie allerdings skeptisch gegenüber, denn auch ihre Meinung über die Māori war in der Vergangenheit von eigenen Beobachtungen und diversen Zeitungsartikeln negativ geprägt worden. Da es an der Zeit war mir einen Eindruck von dem Ort zu machen, der als Basis für meine Recherchen dienen sollte, kontaktierte ich Tokowhā, um mit ihm einen Termin in seinem Haus in Te Kuiti zu vereinbaren.

Als ich mich mit meiner Mutter ein paar Tage später auf den Weg nach Te Kuiti machte, zeigte sich das Wetter nicht gerade von seiner charmantesten Seite. Der Himmel war grau und es nieselte leicht. Je weiter wir uns von Auckland entfernten, umso intensiver prasselten die Regentropfen auf die Windschutzscheibe.

Als wir vom State Highway 1 in Richtung Ngāruawāhia* abbogen, riss der Himmel plötzlich auf und der Grauschleier, der lähmend über dem Land gelegen hatte, verschwand. Was eben noch leblos und fad gewirkt hatte schien nun lebendig und strahlend. Die Wolken wurden von einem schwachen Wind getrieben und wenn sie aufeinandertrafen, schoben sie sich zärtlich aneinander vorbei. Das Land wirkte endlos, auf den satten Weiden graste das Vieh und nur hin und wieder wurde die Weite von einem kleinen Punkt unterbrochen, der auf eine menschliche Bebauung schließen ließ. Hier, vor meinen Augen, erstreckte sich das Neuseeland, dem ich bereits bei meinem ersten Besuch verfallen war. Die weitere Fahrt wirkte wie ein buntes Abenteuer und hinter jeder Kurve erwartete uns ein neuer atemberaubender Ausblick. Es schien fast so, als würde die Natur ihr Begrüßungskomitee bereitstellen, das uns wie sehnsüchtig erwartete Gäste bis nach Te Kuiti geleitete.

Das Ortsschild von Te Kuiti passierten wir unbemerkt. Ein zweites, größeres Schild, das die Stadt als „Sheep Shearing Capital of the World" bewarb, fiel uns jedoch sofort ins Auge. Einmal im Jahr wird das Städtchen zum Treffpunkt der weltbesten Schafscherer, die sich dort mit ihren Kon-

---

*Ngāruawāhia ist die Hochburg der Kīngitanga, einer im 18ten Jahrhundert auf die Bildung einer Monarchie ausgerichteten Māori-Bewegung
Die Stadt gilt auch als Sitz des Māori-Königs, bzw. der Māori-Königin

trahenten einen Wettkampf liefern. Höhepunkt der mehrtägigen Veranstaltung ist der „Sheep Run", ein Spektakel, bei dem etwa zweitausend Schafe durch die Hauptstraße gejagt, und dabei von zahllosen Menschen angefeuert werden.

Während meine Mutter im Café Bosco einen Cappuccino trank, bat ich Tokowhā telefonisch um eine Wegbeschreibung. Ein hübsches Haus im viktorianischen Stil, das an dem von ihm betriebenen Campingplatz angrenzte, war sein Zuhause. Tokowhā war sehr freundlich, und nach einer Tasse Tee sowie einer anschließenden Führung durch sein Haus schlug er vor, mich mit zwei Māori-Damen bekanntzumachen. Ich schätzte es sehr, dass Tokowhā bereits bei meinem ersten Besuch in Te Kuiti einen Kontakt zu anderen Māori herstellte und damit eine wichtige Grundlage für meine Arbeit in den kommenden Wochen legte.

Als wir Tokowhā und die beiden Frauen wenig später verließen, fuhren wir langsam die Hauptstraße Te Kuitis entlang. Sollte die kleine Stadt wirklich einmal einen wirtschaftlichen Aufschwung erlebt haben, dann war dieser lange vorbei. Viele Ladengeschäfte standen leer und außer einer Postfiliale, einem Supermarkt und ein paar Fast-Food-Restaurants hatte Te Kuiti nicht viel zu bieten. Meine Begeisterung über die Aussicht mehrere Wochen hier zubringen zu müssen, hielt sich daher in Grenzen. Meine Mutter und ich tauschten einen kurzen Blick und hatten im Moment nur einen Wunsch: Wir wollten nach Auckland zurück und zwar sofort.

*

Die Koffer waren bereits im Auto verstaut und noch ein letztes Mal genossen wir vom Balkon unseres Motels die Aussicht auf den Sky Tower und die kleinen Inseln, die friedlich im Hauraki Golf vor Auckland lagen. Meine Mutter hatte sich bereit erklärt, mich nach Te Kuiti zu bringen, bevor sie heute um Mitternacht nach Deutschland zurückfliegen würde. Für sie war es ein Abschied von unbestimmter Dauer, für mich bedeutete er den Beginn der zweiten Etappe meiner Reise. Als wir ein paar Minuten später auf den Southern Motorway auffuhren, war meine Gefühlslage geteilt. Auf der einen Seite vermisste ich Auckland, kaum dass wir die Innenstadt verlassen hatten, auf der anderen Seite freute ich mich darauf, endlich mit meinem Projekt zu beginnen.

Im Gegensatz zu unserer ersten Fahrt nach Te Kuiti schenkten wir der malerischen Landschaft dieses Mal kaum Aufmerksamkeit. Die Stimmung war stattdessen von den mittelschweren Spuren einer Melancholie geprägt, in der wir noch einmal die Stationen unserer gemeinsamen Reise Revue passieren ließen. Treffend fasste meine Mutter unsere Empfindungen für Auckland mit den Worten zusammen: „Ich glaube so lange wir leben, werden wir nie von dieser Stadt loskommen!"

Als wir nach knapp drei Stunden Fahrt in Te Kuiti ankamen, war Tokowhā nicht da. Meine Mutter ließ kritisch ihren Blick schweifen und stellte überdies noch unangenehme Fragen: „Bist du dir sicher, dass du hier bleiben willst? Schau dich um, hier gibt es nichts! Hast du wenigstens ein Auto um von hier weg zu kommen?" Sie hatte Recht, im Vergleich zu Auckland gab es in Te Kuiti nichts und sollte mich plötzlich die Verzweiflung packen, dann wusste ich noch nicht einmal, ob und wie ich aus dem Städtchen entkommen konnte. Was sollte ich tun, wenn Tokowhā gar keine Zeit hatte um mir bei meinen Recherchen zu helfen oder schlimmer noch, meine Ankunft einfach vergessen hatte? Obwohl ich in der Regel dazu neige, bei meinen Planungen überorganisiert zu sein, hatte ich in diesem Fall keine Alternative parat. Entweder kehrte ich mit meiner Mutter nach Auckland zurück um mich dort irgendwie durchzuschlagen oder ich blieb hier und vertraute darauf, dass sich alles finden würde. Die wildesten Szenarien geisterten in meinem Kopf herum und brachten mich beinahe zum Strauchen, doch bevor es dazu kam, fuhr Tokowhā mit seinem Jeep auf den Hof. Nach einer herzlichen Begrüßung wies er mich an ihm zu folgen und quartierte mich im schönsten Zimmer im Haus ein.

Mit Tokowhās Erscheinen und seinem entschiedenen Vorgehen waren die Würfel gefallen, Te Kuiti würde von nun an die Basis für mein Buchprojekt sein.

Am Abend hatte ich Gelegenheit, ein erstes intensives Gespräch mit meinem Gastgeber zu führen. Zu meiner Freude hatte Tokowhā bereits Pläne für mich gemacht und für den folgenden Tag einen Interview-Termin mit dem jungen Māori-Künstler Daniel Ormsby aus Waitomo arrangiert.

In Tokowhās Haus standen den Gästen drei Fremdenzimmer zur Verfügung. Weitere Unterkünfte boten die kleinen Cabins, die auf dem Gelände des Campingplatzes verstreut lagen. Bereits innerhalb kürzester Zeit musste ich feststellen, dass Tokowhās Haus nicht gerade der ruhigste Platz auf Erden war. Mit der Ankunft weiterer Gäste, inklusive einer Familie mit drei Kindern, war die Küche permanent belagert und auch der Lärmpegel war dramatisch angestiegen.

Die Menschen, die sich in Tokowhās Haus aufhielten, waren ausnahmslos europäischer Abstammung, alle waren irgendwie spirituell angehaucht oder versuchten zumindest es zu sein. Die meisten von ihnen glichen Booten ohne Kurs, dümpelten auf dem Meer des Lebens umher und suchten sowohl Ziel als auch Richtung. Tokowhā sollte ihnen bei ihrer Orientierungsreise behilflich sein und in Einzelsitzungen bemühte er sich darum, die Gestrandeten wieder auf den richtigen Weg zu bringen. Darüber hinaus wandte er beträchtliche finanzielle Mittel dafür auf, ihnen den Aufenthalt so angenehm wie möglich zu gestalten.

Bei den Māori ist die Gastfreundschaft ein zentraler Pfeiler der Kultur, und Tokowhā wurde seiner Rolle als Gastgeber in vorbildlicher Weise gerecht. Wie selbstverständlich bot er seinen Gästen eine Unterkunft, versorgte sie mit Mahlzeiten, stellte seine Fahrzeuge zur Verfügung und organisierte Ausflüge, in denen er den Besuchern sowohl die Naturschönheiten des Landes als auch die Māori-Kultur näherbrachte. Geduldig schrubbte der Hausherr seine Küche, die oftmals einem wahren Schlachtfeld glich, nachdem die Gäste sie verlassen hatten, und auch wenn die Kinder bis spät in die Nacht im Hausflur herumtobten, ertrug er all das mit einer bewundernswerten Nonchalance. Anstatt um mehr Respekt für sein Haus und sein Habe zu bitten, versuchte Tokowhā seine Gäste durch sein eigenes gutes Beispiel zu sensibilisieren.

Raubbau an einer Kultur

Während meiner Gespräche mit den Māori stellte ich fest, dass vor allem die ältere Generation noch immer darunter leidet, in das Korsett der europäischen Kultur hineingezwängt worden zu sein. Ein Korsett, das sie einschnürte und beschnitt und das ihnen weder heute noch zu Beginn des 19. Jahrhunderts passte, als die ersten Siedler ins Land kamen. Über die Jahre hinweg wurde das Leben der Māori komplett umgestülpt, Anpassung war das Wort der Zeit. Die Expansion der neuen Kultur zeigte sich gnadenlos, nahm weder Rücksicht auf die Gefühle noch auf die Wertvorstellungen der Māori.

Die Māori hatten immer von dem gelebt, was das Land und das Meer ihnen zur Verfügung stellte. Als man ihre Ländereien mit hohen Steuern belegte, konnten viele Māori diese nicht bezahlen. Die Regierung ging dazu über, Māori-Land zu konfiszieren, wodurch man die Menschen automatisch um ihre Lebensgrundlage brachte. Ohne eigenes Land und begrenzte Zugänge zum Meer waren vor allem nach dem Zweiten Weltkrieg immer mehr Māori gezwungen in die Städte zu ziehen, um sich dort nach Arbeit umzusehen. Als erste Auswirkung davon brachen die Sippen auseinander, die Grundlage der Māori-Familien und eine wichtige Institution innerhalb der Māori-Kultur.

Vor allem in den Schulen kam es zu einer Art Umerziehung, wobei die Relevanz der europäischen Kultur gestärkt, die der Māori-Kultur systematisch unterminiert wurde. Mit der Begründung, dass klassische Māori-Namen in der Aussprache zu kompliziert seien, war man in den Schulen dazu übergegangen diese durch europäische zu ersetzen. Als die englische Sprache und die europäische Kultur in der Gesellschaft Neuseelands immer mehr zu dominieren begann, schien plötzlich auch die Māori-Sprache überflüssig zu sein. Ab dem Jahr 1867 wurde Māori in den Schulen zur geächteten Sprache und wer von den Schülern wagte die Sprache zu gebrauchen, der wurde bestraft. Diese angespannte Situation herrschte selbst in den 1950er Jahren noch vor.

Ihres Landes, ihrer Namen und ihrer Sprache beraubt, kam es bei vielen Māori zum Verlust der Identität. Der Ausdruck „verlorene Generation", den viele Māori auf sich anwenden, die in dieser Zeit aufgewachsen sind, beschreibt deutlich den Zwiespalt in dem sie sich befinden. Die Tragik dieser Generation liegt darin, dass sie nicht genau weiß wo sie eigentlich hingehört, die weder in der Māori-Kultur, noch in der Europäischen Kultur zuhause ist.

Es war verständlich, dass die Māori diesen Teil ihrer Vergangenheit am liebsten vergessen wollten und nur ungern darüber sprachen. Ich fühlte mit diesen Menschen und wollte nicht jemand sein, der seine Finger in die alten Wunden legt.

Auch mein Gastgeber Tokowhā war als Kind Opfer entwürdigender Praktiken der Pākehā geworden und litt noch immer unter deren Folgen. Nach seinen eigenen Angaben hatte er den Tod immer wieder gejagt und herausgefordert. Er war ihm hinterher gefahren als er auf Skiern gesperrte Loipen hinabjagte und in selbstmörderischer Geschwindigkeit mit dem Auto über Neuseelands enge Straßen fegte. Doch der Tod hatte ihn nicht gewollt und irgendwann fand sich mein Gastgeber mit dieser Tatsache ab. Auch in Tokowhās Fall gab es ganz sicher einen Zusammenhang zwischen dem Verlust von Kultur und Identität und dem Spiel mit dem Tod.

Leider boten sich mir während meines gesamten Aufenthalts in Neuseeland nicht viele Möglichkeiten mich mit Tokowhā über sein persönliches Schicksal und seine Kultur zu unterhalten. Entweder platzte schon nach kurzer Zeit jemand ins Zimmer und beendete das Gespräch, oder er war so müde, dass ihm schon nach wenigen Minuten die Augen zufielen. „Später", pflegte er zu sagen, während er auf seinem Sessel ins Reich der Träume entschwand.

Doch auch wenn es bei Tokowhās Versprechen blieb, diverse Dinge später nachzuholen so tat er stets sein Bestes, mich mit interessanten Gesprächspartnern zu versorgen. Wann immer er für seine Besucher Ausflüge organisierte, bot er mir an mitzukommen, und während seine Gäste durch den Regenwald stiefelten und sich beim Wildwasser-Rafting oder beim Bungy-Jumping ihren Adrenalinstoß holten, chauffierte Tokowhā mich von einem Interviewpartner zum nächsten.

ie Rückkehr eines Volkes

Vor meiner Reise nach Neuseeland stellte ich mir in Bezug auf die Māori viele Fragen. Ich war neugierig herauszufinden, ob diese Menschen tatsächlich in die Schublade passten, in die ich sie vor vielen Jahren gesteckt hatte.

Deutliche Antworten erhielt ich während des „Carving-Weekend", das Ostern auf dem Gelände der Schule Kura Kaupapa Māori in Ōparure stattfand. In einem Zeitraum von sechzig Stunden wollten vierzehn Künstler zwei große Holzpfähle, Totempfählen gleich, schnitzen und auf dem Schulgelände errichten. Unterstützt wurden sie dabei von den Lehrern sowie vielen Freiwilligen.

Nachdem ich mit allen Anwesenden bekannt gemacht worden war, fühlte ich mich wie der Offizier John Dunbar in dem Film „Der mit dem Wolf tanzt". Bei seinem ersten Besuch bei den Sioux hatte Dunbar überrascht festgestellt, dass nichts, was man ihm über die Indianer erzählt hatte, der Wahrheit entsprach. Die Sioux waren keine grausamen Wilden, sondern humorvolle, familienorientierte und naturliebende Menschen. Hier, im Kreis der Māori, erlebte ich dasselbe wie John Dunbar. Ich begegnete Menschen, die offen und gastfreundlich waren, die sich mit gegenseitigem Respekt behandelten, die fleißig arbeiteten und die keinerlei Misstrauen gegen mich hegten. Geduldig erläuterten sie mir Einzelheiten zu ihrer Kultur, und als ich ihnen von meinem Projekt erzählte, boten mir einige sogar ihre Unterstützung an. All die schlechten Eigenschaften, die ich zwei Jahrzehnte lang als Synonym für die Māori gesehen hatte, erwiesen sich als völlig unpassend. Unter all den liebenswürdigen Menschen schämte ich mich für die Vorurteile, die ich so lange kultiviert und gepflegt hatte, ohne sie jemals zu hinterfragen.

Während meines Aufenthalts in Neuseeland zählten aber nicht nur Māori zu meinen Gesprächspartnern, ich war auch an dem interessiert was die Pākehā zu sagen hatten. Wie schon vor zwanzig Jahren beschwerten sich einige darüber, dass sich die Māori in den vergangenen Jahrhunderten die europäische Kultur nicht wirklich zu Eigen gemacht haben und stattdessen weiterhin ihre eigenen Bräuche pflegen. Ist es unangebracht die Frage zu stellen, ob sich die Pākehā in der Vergangenheit jemals die Kultur der Māori zu Eigen gemacht haben, waren sie es doch, die in ein fremdes Land eingefallen sind?

Wenn man die Geschichte betrachtet dann muss man leider feststellen, dass die eingewanderten Europäer lange Zeit keinen einzigen Teil der Māori-Kultur als kostbar genug erachtet haben um ihn zu bewahren. Wen wundert es daher, dass der Umgang zwischen Māori und Pākehā noch immer von Misstrauen geprägt ist? Die Ereignisse der Vergangenheit haben sich in die Seelen der Māori eingebrannt wie Brandzeichen. Noch viele Generationen und die Bereitschaft zu vergeben sind nötig, um die Schmerzen, die mit der Erinnerung an diese dunklen Zeiten verbunden sind, zu lindern.

Seit den 1960er Jahren haben die Māori immer häufiger ihren Unmut gegen die ihnen auferlegten Beschränkungen kundgetan. Einige Māori wurden zu Symbolfiguren des Aufstandes, so wie die Aktivistin Whina Cooper, die im Alter von zweiundachtzig Jahren den berühmten „Māori-Landmarsch von 1975" anführte. Der 29 Tage dauernde Protestmarsch für die Landrechte der Māori begann am 14. September 1975 in Te Hāpua, an der Nordspitze Neuseelands und führte bis in die tausend Kilometer entfernte Hauptstadt Wellington. Am 13. Oktober 1975 erreichte Whina Cooper mit dem etwa fünftausend Menschen zählenden Protestzug Wellington und übergab an die Regierung und das Neuseeländische Parlament das „Memorial of Right"* sowie eine von 60.000 Menschen unterzeichnete Petition.

Im Jahr 1975 wurde das Waitangi Tribunal eingerichtet, eine Instanz, die den Māori hilft ihre Rechtsansprüche, die sich aus dem Treaty of Waitangi ableiten lassen, geltend zu machen. Zwischenzeitlich haben die Māori auch das Recht auf ihre Sprache wiedererlangt, und seit 1987 ist Māori neben Englisch offizielle Amtssprache Neuseelands. Durch ihre Beharrlichkeit ist es den Māori in den letzten Jahrzehnten gelungen, ihre Kultur im eigenen Land wieder zu etablieren. Weltweit genießt die Māori-Kultur ein hohes Ansehen, weshalb jedes Jahr Hunderttausende nach Aotearoa reisen um einen Einblick in die Lebensart und die traditionsreiche Geschichte der Māori zu erhalten.

Dieses Buch reicht nicht aus, um alle Facetten der Māori-Kultur zu beleuchten, trotzdem hoffe ich, dass es Ihnen Freude bereitet, mit mir auf den nachfolgenden Seiten einen Streifzug durch die faszinierende und einzigartige Welt der Māori zu unternehmen.

*Das „Memorial of Right" enthielt zwei politische Forderungen, in denen die Māori Entscheidungsfreiheit bei der Verwaltung ihrer Ländereien sowie die Beendigung der Konfiszierung von Māori-Land forderten

Desire is Incurable

Stories often have strange beginnings and this one started with the search for an alibi - an alibi that would allow me a three month stay in New Zealand.

My previous visits there had been holidays in which I had explored the country and enjoyed the wide beaches. When I first arrived in Auckland on the North Island in the early 1990s New Zealand immediately crept into my heart and cast its anchor.

What about *Māori**, the indigenous people of New Zealand, you may ask? At that time my knowledge about them was no more than what can be read in any guidebook and to be honest, I was not really interested in their history or fate. I was fascinated by New Zealand's landscape, the snow-capped mountains, the impenetrable rain forests, the rushing waterfalls, the silence and solitude that was immediately available when I longed for it.

At some point during my trip I had visited the Waitangi Treaty Grounds in Paihia, a historic place where in the year 1840 the Treaty of Waitangi had been signed, an agreement that was set up to guarantee the Māori and the immigrant settlers a peaceful coexistence in *Aotearoa* (the Māori name for New Zealand). Years of brutal wars, that had claimed a high death toll on both sides, had preceded the treaty. The British had invaded the country, determined to take what they wanted, Māori land. Those who did not cooperate by giving the land voluntarily were expropriated or convinced by force of arms. However, the hopes that had been expected of the Treaty of Waitangi had not been fulfilled and the battles between Europeans and Māori continued for many more years. Nowadays on the Waitangi Treaty Grounds a thirty-foot war canoe (*waka taua*) and a beautifully carved meeting house (*whare hui)* are symbols of the Māori culture. Those who would rightfully expect that I encountered numerous Māori during my stay on the site are mistaken I didn't meet a single person who was Māori.

I sourced information about Māori from daily newspapers, which regularly reported offenses committed by them; the unemployment rate among Māori was high and only a few attained a qualification of higher education. When I talked with the local *Pākehā* (New Zealanders of European descent) I realised, that they did not speak with too much enthusiasm about their indigenous neighbours. Disputes about land and property were on the daily agenda, the Pākehā complained about the reluctance of Māori to adapt to their Western culture and their refusal to see its benefits.

While I was traveling New Zealand regrettably too often, the newspaper articles and the evalu-

*All terms from the Māori language are explained in the glossary

ation of European residents seemed to be confirmed. When I passed Māori settlements they mostly looked messy and unkempt. Overweight people sat on their terraces or hung around in the streets, smoking and drinking beer. Some of them wore tattoos, either on their faces or spread over a large area of their bodies. The houses were neglected, the gardens overgrown and I got the impression that physical work was not a favourite activity of these people. Most of the families seemed to be blessed with plenty of children, however instead of taking the responsibility to provide for their needs they preferred to rely on the government's help, content to receive a weekly benefit. In addition reports about violent gangs added fear and terror amongst the citizens. All these things did not paint a bright picture of Māori and after all the things I had seen and heard, I felt absolutely no desire to get in touch with them.

I must admit I was full of prejudice, prejudice against people I didn't even know. At best, I had once been with a Māori in the 'Fish and chips shop' waiting for an order and even that without talking a single word. My enthusiasm was limited to the country of Aotearoa that day after day injected me a new dose of its sweet poison. I wanted more and more of it and when I had to return back to Germany after five weeks I was an addict, constantly obsessed with the idea of returning to Aotearoa as soon as possible. Over the following years I visited New Zealand several times but never came in personal contact with Māori.

*

Now, almost twenty years since my first visit the idea has settled in my head to get to know the Māori people and to write about them. You may well ask, "What led to this change of heart?"

Let me explain it this way: Aotearoa had never let me go and every return trip caused me real pain. When the plane spit me out in a German airport after nearly thirty hours travel time I felt inwardly robbed. As I pulled the suitcase from the baggage carousel, my heart was still in New Zealand and made no attempt to unite with me here in Germany; to return to my normal life was extremely difficult and usually took me several weeks.

One day I was completely fed up with this unsatisfactory situation and when the opportunity came up to change my job situation, I grabbed it. As a journalist I had much more leeway, was no longer bound regionally and more flexible to take even longer journeys. New Zealand came within reach again, but this time I would not be content with a short stay of just a couple of weeks. To travel the country for several months without a plan was still not easily possible, unless there was something specific that would justify my presence.

And there it was again: the search for an alibi. However, to hide several months behind a poor alibi was not my style, I needed a mission. A book project that required a long time for field research seemed to be the perfect plan. The longer I thought about the idea the more I liked it, but what should I write about? Already too much had been written about the history of New Zealand, its conquest by the British and their conflict with Māori.

When I considered my attitude to the Māori I came to the conclusion, that I owed them a neutral and impartial attitude. My evaluation of these people was based on what I had heard, read or seen. None of this had I verified in a personal conversation with a Māori. I had always concentrated on the country and by that I forgot its people. I had no idea of Māori, but how could I even begin to claim to know a country if I did not know any of its indigenous people? How could I claim to love a country, unless I loved its indigenous people? However, before I could love them I had to get to know them. One thing was not possible without the other.

But was I even qualified enough to cope with a project of this kind, competent enough to write about a culture I knew absolutely nothing about? Before I started planning I decided to review my motives and qualifications.

I pride myself on having a clear mind, the willingness to fill my heart with honest impressions and an ability to write from the abundance of it. In addition, I am curious about everything and with my eternal questioning in my search for answers I can be a true pain in the neck. What I like most about being a journalist is the search for the truth through background research and investigation. From past experience I found the truth is not always easily forthcoming. I know some journalists have compromised to the point where they'd write what their conversation partners wanted them to write.

Would I imitate them in this book? The answer to this question would depend on my motivation. Would it be my goal to try to please somebody or was I solely focused on searching for the truth? The search for the truth that would hurt sometimes; I've found finding the truth was never a painless endeavour. In this research, many emotions would be involved, which would automatically lead to painful memories. Often, long built-up resentment could be washed to the surface. How would the Māori engage with me in conversation? How would they view my questions? Would they put me into the same drawer as Pākehā, the people who had deprived them of their land and who had murdered their ancestors?

Even if I was confident enough with this project, I first had to make contact with the Māori. When I looked at it realistically I was about 20 000 kilometres away from a Māori person - not really a good starting situation. The only possibility to get in contact with these people was to connect with a Māori organization via the Internet.

To start I returned to the place where in 1992 I had my first cautious contact with the Māori culture, the Waitangi National Trust in Paihia. After several weeks the organization told me via e-mail that after careful consideration they had come to the conclusion that they could neither support me with my project nor be able to help me to get in contact with Māori families; another organization that I had written to at the same time, didn't answer at all. Disappointed I searched the Internet for more contact points, but without success. It seemed that my project would fail before it had even started.

A few days later fate came to my aid in the form of an event note. Just around the corner from the little town where I lived a Māori visitor wanted to give a presentation about New Zealand. Incredulously I stared at the small note that promised me what I was looking for, a Māori.

 First Encounter

A considerable number of people had accepted the invitation to attend the photo show with the title "New Zealand - the land of the Māori". I knew that it would not be good for me to see pictures of New Zealand, as this would immediately create the urgent desire to pack my bags and to drive to the nearest airport. Therefore my plan was to make contact with this Māori person before the event even started and then to disappear through the next door. When I arrived however, the stage was empty, no trace of the Māori speaker anywhere. Although I didn't like it I had to find a seat and wait. After about ten minutes a man, dressed in jeans and a sweater, came into the room. "My name is Tokowhā and I'm from New Zealand", he said in broken German. Shortly after his introduction he presented images of New Zealand's landscape. There and then the spirit captured me, pulled me along and once again, for me anyway there was absolutely no escape.

When the slide show came to an end, Tokowhā took the audience on a journey into his childhood of the 1950s. He told how he had been robbed of his name by his Pākehā teacher and how he was given the name "John". Pointing at the scar that was visible on his brow, he reported how he had been mistreated in school because he had spoken Māori instead of English. During these difficult times he had received support from his great-grandfather, who encouraged him again and again to be proud of his Māori roots. The fate of this little boy, who had to go through all this because he was from the "wrong" race and had the "wrong" skin colour, deeply touched me.

When it came to a break I was truly relieved and went straight up to meet this man. Without much preface I said: "My name is Claudia, I am a journalist and would like to write about your people." The Māori first remained silent and piercingly looked at me with his black eyes, as if he was trying to check my motives. Then he finally said, "Come to my home in New Zealand and

write about my people."

I left the hall with a business card in my hands before the second part of the event started. I could hardly believe what had happened in the last couple of minutes. This encounter with Tokowhā would open my way to travel to New Zealand in order to realise my book idea. I did not know at that time when I would start the trip, but knew I would move heaven and earth to ensure it would happen soon.

The next evening I wrote an e-mail to Tokowhā and thanked him for his offer to help me with the book. He wanted to stay a few weeks more in Germany and it would have been good for me to meet up with him again to get more insight into the plight of the Māori. Tokowhā tried to schedule a meeting with me, but it wasn't to be, he flew back to New Zealand in October.

I was carefully nursing Tokowhā's business card like a precious gem. A whole year passed on in which I tried to stay in touch with him via e-mail. Tokowhā didn't write often, and when he did, it was usually only a few words. Despite this, I was happy whenever he replied, even if he only replied out of courtesy. It may sound dramatic, but I had to rely on this man, without him the realisation of this book would not have been possible.

When summer came in Germany Tokowhā informed me by e-mail that he would soon be arriving. Since it was nearing time to specify my travel plans, I was quite keen in meeting up with him. A few days later he stood at my front door. I don't remember in detail what he told me, but it was too much for a person you've just met. He spoke softly, almost toneless, and occasionally, when the darkness of the past laid its shadow, his face was bathed in pain. When he left a couple of hours later I sat still in complete silence for a while to take in all that he'd shared.

Tokowhā had caught my curiosity and the following evening I invited him for dinner. However, even though he had promised to come, he didn't show up, no call, and no message. Was this unreliability a part of the Māori culture? Was it a foretaste of what I could expect in New Zealand? He eventually showed up a day later and didn't even mention missing our previous engagement. When I asked him about it he only said: "At night I don't eat anyway". Within the next few hours he took me on another journey into his past once again.

This further encounter with Tokowhā encouraged me to travel back to New Zealand as soon as possible. Although I still had no information about how my stay in Tokowhā's house would be, I searched the Internet for a suitable flight. Without thinking twice I booked my departure for mid-January.

Three months before the scheduled departure I started packing my bags, a clear indication that I could hardly wait to leave Germany. To improve my meagre knowledge of the Māori culture I purchased books, which I eagerly devoured, but what I read was not in the least adequate to give

Pōhutu Geyser in the Whakarewarewa Thermal Valley in Rotorua, North Island
Pōhutu Geysir in dem geothermischen Areal Whakarewarewa in Rotorua, Nordinsel

me a clear picture of Māori people. There was nothing else to do but keep my curiosity in check and to wait patiently for the day of my departure.

Finally, New Zealand

The rain forest was a magical place I loved to roam. The sky was barely visible through the dense netting of leaves, the birds that swayed in the wind in the treetop chirped happily, and the cicadas started to sing their melody. It was like they all together wanted to encourage me to finally start my journey into the unknown world of Māori.

I'd been in New Zealand for several days. My mother, who many years earlier had also lost her heart to this country, accompanied me for the first three weeks. She viewed my book project with huge scepticism as her opinion of Māori had also been negatively influenced in the past, either by her own observations or by various media prejudice. Understandably she was keen on meeting the man who would provide me with accommodation for the next couple of weeks. Because it was time for me to take a closer look at the place that would serve as the basis for my research I contacted Tokowhā to schedule an appointment with him at his home in Te Kuiti.

When we made our way down to Te Kuiti a couple of days later, the weather wasn't the best. The sky was grey and it was slightly drizzling. The further we got away from Auckland, the more intensely the raindrops pelted on the windscreen.

As we turned off from State Highway 1 towards Ngāruawāhia* the sky opened up and suddenly the grey veil, that had been paralyzing the country for quite a while, disappeared. What had been lifeless and dull now seemed alive and radiant. The clouds were chased by a light wind and when they collided, they tenderly pushed against each other like lovers. The country seemed endless, the cattle grazed on the lush pastures and only occasionally the expanse was interrupted by small dots, which seemed to be human constructions. Here, in front of my eyes, the New Zealand I had already been fallen for on my first visit spread out in its full beauty.

The rest of the journey seemed to be like a colourful adventure and behind every corner a new beautiful view surprised us. Nature seemed to provide its welcoming committee, treating us like eagerly awaited guests, escorting us down to Te Kuiti.

Unnoticed we entered the little town Te Kuiti. A large name plate caught our eye immediately, honouring the city as "Sheep Shearing Capital of the World". Once a year the world's best sheep

*Ngāruawāhia is the stronghold of the Kīngitanga, a Māori Movement that was founded in the 18th century to establish a Māori political model to offset the introduced Pākehā monarchy. It is also the official residence of the Māori King or Queen

shearers are coming to Te Kuiti to compete for the title. Highlight of the multi-day event is the "Sheep Run", a spectacle in which about two thousand sheep are chased down the main street, and whooped by countless people.

While my mother was sipping a cappuccino in the Bosco-Café, I called Tokowhā on the phone to get the directions. A pretty Victorian-style house, which bordered on the campground that he operated, was his home. Tokowhā was very friendly and after a cup of tea and a short tour through his house, he suggested making contact with two Māori women. I appreciated it very much that already during my first visit Tokowhā arranged a contact with other Māori laying an important foundation for my literary work.

Later, after we left Tokowhā and the two women we drove slowly along the main road of Te Kuiti. If the small town ever had experienced an economic boom, then it was long gone. Many shops were empty and except for a post office, a supermarket and a few fast food restaurants Te Kuiti had little to offer. My mother and I looked at each other and without saying a word we had the same wish: we wanted to go back to Auckland immediately.

*

The bags were already packed and stored in the boot of the car and for the last time we stood on the balcony of our motel enjoying the view on Auckland's Sky Tower looking at the small islands that lay peacefully in the Hauraki Gulf. My mother had agreed to take me down to Te Kuiti, before she flew back to Germany at midnight. For her it was a goodbye for an indefinite time, for me it meant the beginning of the second stage of my journey. When we entered the Southern Motorway a few minutes later, my feelings were divided. On one hand, despite barely having left the city, I missed Auckland, but on the other hand, I was looking forward to starting my project.

Compared to our first trip to Te Kuiti this time we only gave the picturesque landscape a little attention. Instead our mood was dominated by moderate traces of melancholy in which we recalled the stop-overs of our previous week's holiday. Appropriately my mother summed up our feelings for Auckland, saying: "I think as long as we live, we'll never get away from this city!"

When we arrived in Te Kuiti after a journey of almost three hours, Tokowhā was not there. My mother, who had to immediately drive back to Auckland, allowed her gaze to wander around critically and asked the unpleasant question. "Are you really sure that you want to stay here? Have a look around! There is nothing, not even a car to get away if you want to!" She was right, in comparison to Auckland there was nothing here and should sudden despair take hold of me, I did not even know whether and how I could escape. What should I do if Tokowhā would not have the time to help me with my research or even worse had forgotten my arrival? Although in general I

Next page: Auckland, North Island
My travel vehicle during my time of research
Mein Reisegefährt während meiner Recherchen

am always over-organized with my activities, in this case I didn't have a plan B. It was up to me now; I could return to Auckland to battle my way there or stay here in Te Kuiti hoping that everything would be fine. The wildest scenarios haunted my thoughts and almost made me stumble, but before that happened, a cheerful Tokowhā arrived, asked me to follow him and put me into the loveliest room in the house. With Tokowhā's arrival and his decisive action, the die was cast: from now on Te Kuiti would be the basis for my book project.

In the evening I had my first deep conversation with my host. Tokowhā had already made plans for me and the following day he had made an appointment with the young Māori artist Daniel Ormsby from Waitomo who would introduce me to the subject of *Tā moko*, the traditional art of Māori tattooing.

In Tokowhā's house there were three guest rooms; further accommodation was offered in the form of small cabins, which were scattered on the grounds of the campsite. Within a very short time I realised that Tokowhā's house was not the quietest place on earth. With the arrival of other guests, including a family with three children, the kitchen was constantly besieged and the noise level had increased dramatically. The people who were staying in Tokowhā's house were without exception of European descent. They were all kind of spiritual or at least tried to be that way. Most of them seemed like boats without a course, bobbing up and down on the sea of life, looking for both, a goal and a direction. Tokowhā was willing to support them on their journey and in individual sessions he tried to bring the stranded back on the right track. Beyond that Tokowhā invested a significant amount of money to make the stay of his guests as pleasant as possible.

Hospitality is a central pillar of the culture and Tokowhā filled his role as host in an exemplary manner. Naturally, he offered the people accommodation and provided them with meals and vehicles. He also organized tours, showing them the natural beauties of the country as well as allowing them insights into the Māori culture. Patiently my host scrubbed his kitchen that often, after the guests had left, looked as devastated as a battlefield and while the children were frolicking until late at night in the hallway, he endured all with an admirable nonchalance. Instead of asking for more respect for his house and his belongings, Tokowhā tried to sensitise his guests by his good example.

*

During my conversations with Māori, I realised that the older generation in particular is still suffering from being forced into the corset of European culture, a corset that didn't fit, that constricted and circumcised them. Since the arrival of the British the world of the Māori was completely shattered; - adaptation was survival. The expansion of the new culture was merciless and showed no consideration for the feelings or values of Māori.

Māori had always lived from the bounty of land and sea. When the land was burdened with taxes many Māori were not able to pay and their land was confiscated. By taking away the land Māori automatically lost their sense of well being and identity. Without land and having only a limited access to the sea Māori became dispossessed. Post World War II Māori people were urbanised into cities to look for work. An immediate impact was that the extended family structures that underpinned the family (*whānau*) structure of Māori broke apart.

This was especially evident in schools where a sort of re-education took place whereby the relevance of the Pākehā culture had been strengthened and whereby the relevance of Māori culture was systematically undermined. With the explanation that Māori names were too complicated to pronounce, schools started to replace them with European ones. When they did use Māori names they were often misspelt and consequently mispronounced. When the English language and the European culture increasingly started to dominate within New Zealand society it became a popular convention that the Māori language was no longer necessary. From the year 1867, Te reo Māori was declared a banned language in schools and those who dared to use it, were punished. This tense situation prevailed even in the 1950s.

Deprived of their land, their names and their language, a lot of Māori people lost their identity. The term "lost generation" that many Māori who grew up during that time apply to themselves clearly describes the dilemma they are in. The tragedy of this generation lies in the fact that they do not know where they actually belong, not feeling at home in the Māori culture, or in the Pākehā culture.

It was understandable that Māori wanted to forget these dark times speaking only reluctantly of their experiences. I felt for these people and really did not want to be the one poking around in old wounds.

As a child even my host Tokowhā was a victim of the degrading practices of the Pākehā and he is still suffering from those consequences. According to his own statements he had chased and challenged death for a long time. He went after death as he raced down blocked ski trails or by speeding his car with suicidal intent over New Zealand's treacherously narrow roads. However, death didn't want him and finally my host accepted this. In his case, there was certainly a connection between the loss of culture and identity and the temptation to gamble with death.

Unfortunately, during my entire stay in New Zealand there were only a few opportunities to talk with my host Tokowhā about Māori culture. Either someone bounced into the room after a short time ending the conversation or Tokowhā was so tired that he couldn't keep his eyes open.

"Later", he used to say, while he fell asleep in his chair, but even if he didn't manage to keep his promises to do the postponed things later, he always did his best to provide me with interesting interview partners. Whenever he organised trips for his visitors, he offered me to come along. While his guests were striding through the rain forest or getting their adrenaline boost while white water rafting or bungee jumping, Tokowhā chauffeured me from one interview partner to another.

People Returning

Before my trip to New Zealand, I asked myself a lot of questions about Māori. I was curious to find out whether Māori really fitted into the drawer where I had put them during all those earlier years while I had travelled their country.

I received all the answers to these questions while I was attending a "Carving Weekend" which took place during Easter on the campus of the school Kura Kaupapa Māori in Ōparure. Within a time frame of sixty hours fourteen well-known artists wanted to carve two large piles of wood, similar to totem poles and erect them on the school grounds. The carvers were supported by the school staff and by many volunteers. After I was introduced to all the attendants, I felt like the officer John Dunbar in the film "Dances with Wolves". During his first visit to the Sioux Dunbar was surprised to find out that nothing he had been told about the red Indians was true. The Sioux were not cruel savages, but humorous, family-oriented and nature-loving people. The same happened to me here in the midst of the Māori. I was surrounded by open and hospitable people that treated each other with mutual respect and worked together peacefully. Patiently they explained details of their culture to me and as I told them about my project, some of them offered their support. All the bad qualities that I had seen as a synonym for the Māori for almost twenty years proved to be completely inaccurate. Between all these gracious people, I felt embarrassed for the prejudices that I had cultivated and maintained for so long without ever questioning them.

During my stay in New Zealand I not only spoke to Māori people, I was also interested in the opinion of the Pākehā. As in the 1990s some complained that over the last two centuries the Māori have not really adopted the European culture and instead continued to maintain their own customs.

Is it audacious to ask the question whether in the past the Pākehā had ever made the attempt to embrace the Māori culture? Remember, they have been the ones who have invaded a foreign country!

If you look at the history unfortunately it must be said, that for a long time Pākehā did not even view a single aspect of Māori culture as being valuable enough to preserve. Is it any wonder then that the interaction between Māori and Pākehā is still characterized by mistrust? The events of the past are burned into the people's souls like brand marks, many generations and a great deal of understanding are needed to alleviate the pain associated with the memory of these dark times.

Since the 1960s, little by little Māori have loosened the corset of restrictions imposed by European oppression which constrained them for so long. There are significant Māori that can be seen as symbolic figures during the time of revolt. One of them was Whina Cooper, a committed activist, who, at the age of 82 led the famous "Māori land march of 1975", a 29-day protest march for Māori land rights. The walk began on September 4th 1975 in Te Hāpua, on the northern tip of New Zealand, and journeyed down a thousand kilometres to the remote capital of Wellington. On the 13th of October Whina Cooper accompanied by about five thousand people, arrived in the capital where she handed over the "Memorial of Right"* and a petition signed by 60,000 people to the government and the New Zealand Parliament.

In 1975, the Waitangi Tribunal was established that supported Māori to recognise their titles derived under the Treaty of Waitangi. Meanwhile Māori have also regained the right to recognise their language and since 1987 Māori is an official language of New Zealand. Through their persistence in the recent decades Māori managed to re-establish their culture. Throughout the world Māori culture enjoys a positive reputation which motivates hundreds of thousands of people per year to travel to New Zealand Aotearoa to take a closer look at the inspiring culture of Māori.

This book does not have enough pages to show all the facets of Māori culture. Nevertheless, I hope you enjoy joining me on the next pages on a foray through the fascinating and unique world of Māori.

*The "Memorial of Right" included two political demands in which the Māori people asked for autonomy of decision in the management of their land and the termination of the confiscation of Māori land

Next page: Coastal road to Kaikoura, South Island
Nächste Seite: Küstenstraße nach Kaikoura, Südinsel

The Marae —

A Place of Belonging

Te Marae -

He Tūrangawaewae

Marae —

Ein Stück Heimat

He pōkeke Uenuku i tū ai

Against a dark cloud the rainbow stands out brightly

Marae – The Heart of the Māori Culture

What do you associate with the term "home"? Most of us might think of words like "security" and "safety". Home is the place where we belong, where we feel comfortable and where we can find inner peace.

Māori people experience these kinds of feelings of home and closeness when they come back to their *marae*, the traditional gathering place of their people. Although at first glance it appears to be a place for ceremonial greetings, speeches and cultural activities, the marae is much more than that, it is the epitome for the identity of Māori people and represents the heart of Māori culture.

The marae is the place where Māori can be Māori, because there is nowhere else that Māori can be as close to their culture than in the home of their ancestors. The marae combines the existence of every individual with their past, present and future, and therefore it is more than fitting that Māori call the marae their *tūrangawaewae*, their "Place of belonging".

The former leader of the Tūhoe tribe, John Rangiāniwaniwa Rangihau, once explained the importance of the marae for his people as follows:

"Marae are places of refuge for our people,
and provide facilities to enable us to continue with
our own way of life and within the total structure
of our terms and values.
We need a marae for a host of reasons:
that we may rise tall in oratory,
that we may weep for our dead,
that we may pray to God,
that we may house our guests,
that we may have our meetings,
that we may have our weddings,
that we may have our reunions,
that we may sing,
that we may dance,
that we may learn our history, and then know
that richness of life and the proud heritage which is truly ours."

Marae on the North Island
above: Pakake Taiari Marae, Mokai
below: Te Kāwau Maro Tua Rua Marae, Waitomo

In New Zealand there are about eight hundred marae and during my stay, I had many opportunities to visit several of these special places of gathering, the occasions were either to attend funerals, weddings or welcoming ceremonies.

In addition to the meeting house (*whare hui*) you can also find a dining room, a sleeping house, toilets and a cemetery. Although the term "marae" in general only specifies the defined area directly in front of the meeting house, the term is synonymously used to describe the entire area.

Most of the tribes, sub tribes and also smaller Māori communities still have their own marae. The people who belong to the marae are called *tangata whenua*, "people of the land". The behaviour in the marae is determined by a protocol that varies from marae to marae.

In the meeting house for instance you might not be allowed to wear shoes, to smoke, eat or even to use the carvings or pictures as coat hooks. In the dining room you are taught to refrain from sitting on the tables or from holding your plate over the heads of other guests. By observing these protocols you show your respect to the hosts and to Māori cultural traditions. If you are not sure how to behave on the marae, then it is best to orientate yourself on the example of the other people present.

The Pōwhiri

In a formal meeting the *pōwhiri*, or traditional welcome ceremony, is the key to entering onto a marae. Whenever you attend a pōwhiri you will be welcomed by the hosts with dignity and respect. The term *waewae tapu*, "sacred feet", properly describes the precious status that guests hold.

I experienced my first pōwhiri one Easter at a Kura Kaupapa School in Ōparure in connection with a "Carving Weekend". Before the project started the hosts welcomed their guests (*manuhiri*) with a pōwhiri.

That evening along with the many other visitors I gathered outside the gates of the marae. After we had introduced ourselves a prayer (*inoi*) was said, asking for guidance and protection of the people attending. Then we queued up in front of the entrance, women and children first, followed closely by the men.

The forming of the guests in front of the entrance gate is the signal for the hosts to start the pōwhiri.

A pōwhiri involves the following elements:

Karanga	Call of Welcome
Whaikōrero	Speech
Koha	Gift
Hongi	To Press Noses
Hākari	Feast

The pōwhiri was initiated by a call of welcome, the *karanga*. One of the senior women from the ranks of the hosts, stood in front of the meeting house, raising her voice to give a melodic call of welcome from which we slowly began to move onto the marae. Before the first voice died away, a woman from our ranks answered the call. The antiphony, that was so touching and intense that a shiver ran down my spine, lasted until we had arrived in front of the meeting house.

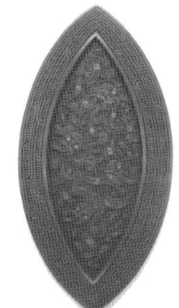

With this first call the marae becomes sacred (tapu). All the other elements of the pōwhiri are focused on removing the tapu of the visitors and making them one with the hosts.

According to the seating plan in the meeting house the men were assigned to the front rows and the women to the back. Within the next hour there was a verbal exchange (*whaikōrero*) between speakers from the group of the hosts returned by a speaker from our group. Both groups alternated in their speeches with a man from the host's side opening the exchange. Only capable orators are bestowed with the privilege to speak on the marae and by using metaphors and parables during their whaikōrero these men can put their oratory skills to the test.

After our speaker had finished his last speech, he placed an envelope that contained a donation (*koha*) in front of the hosts. The purpose of the koha is to assist the hosts with the maintenance of the marae, and to cover the expenses incurred during the gathering (*hui*). In former times it was customary that guests gave items as koha that were of high value in their home regions. Items such as whale bones, seafood delicacies or elaborate woven cloaks would accord prestige (*mana*) to both the giver and the recipient.

When the last speaker on the host side had closed off his speech the rest of the home people would sing a song (*waiata*) to accompany his speech. We were then encouraged to come forward to greet the hosts. Although shaking hands (*harirū*) is part of the greeting, the focus is on the *hongi*, the pressing of nose and forehead. The hongi symbolises the sharing of the breath of life and signifies that life is a gift that comes from the gods. (The execution of this practice varies from region to region.)

After leaving the meeting house, the two groups were brought together in the dining room for the banquet (*hākari*). With this meal, which is usually a *hāngi* (food cooked in the earth oven) the welcome ceremony officially ends. Most important is that with the hākari the state of tapu is lifted from both groups, they become neutral (*noa*) and come together as one united entity as tangata whenua.

Here are the components of the whare hui:

1, Tekoteko:
The carved figure, which is on the roof of the meeting house, symbolises the head of the ancestor

2, Maihi:
The bargeboard represents the outstretched arms of the ancestor, which embrace guests as a gesture of welcome

3, Raparapa:
The extension of the bargeboard symbolises the fingers of the ancestor

4, Amo:
The carved figure on the two pillars represents the two sides of the body of the ancestor

5, Tāhuhu:
The ridge pole in the meeting house symbolises the spine of the ancestor

6, Heke:
The rafters on both sides of the ridge pole embody the ribs of the ancestor

⟡ Look into the Whare Hui

After dinner I took the time to take a closer look at the meeting house. By doing that I had the privilege of having someone at my side who was kind enough to explain the meaning of each component of the building that have huge significance for Māori.

The drawing below shows the meeting house (*whare hui*) or "house of the ancestors" (*whare tūpuna*). When you walk into the whare hui, you do not enter just an ordinary house, rather an old history book or living archive.

In its construction, the whare hui is modelled after a human body, symbolising the body of an ancestor after who the house is named. The building is generously decorated with carvings and inside you will find pictures and photographs of all the deceased of the tribe.

If you should pass a marae during your New Zealand trip and feel the desire to visit the site, please do not hesitate to contact Māori maintaining the marae often living next to the site. In general, the Māori people are pleased about the interest that is given to their culture and enjoy giving visitors an understanding about their marae and its history.

I can´t begin to tell you what opportunity awaits you just by making this simple gesture. Believe me dear readers, the visit to a marae and the associated pōwhiri, is a unique experience you will never forget.

Marae – Das Herz der Māori-Kultur

Was verbinden Sie mit dem Begriff „Heimat"? Den meisten von uns kommen dabei Worte wie Geborgenheit und Sicherheit in den Sinn. Heimat ist der Platz an dem wir glücklich sind, wo wir hingehören und wo wir uns wohlfühlen.

Die meisten Māori verspüren dieses Gefühl von Heimat und Verbundenheit, wenn sie zu ihrem *marae*, der traditionellen Versammlungsstätte ihres Volkes, zurückkehren. Obwohl auf den ersten Blick ein Ort für zeremonielle Begrüßungen, Reden und kulturelle Aktivitäten, ist der Marae viel mehr als das, er ist der Inbegriff für die Identität der Māori und bildet das Herzstück der Māori-Kultur.

Der Marae ist der Ort, an dem ein Māori ein Māori sein kann, denn nirgendwo ist er seiner Kultur näher als im Haus seiner Vorfahren. Im Marae verbindet sich die Existenz jedes Einzelnen mit seiner Vergangenheit, seiner Gegenwart und seiner Zukunft und daher ist es mehr als passend, dass die Māori den Marae als *tūrangawaewae*, den „Platz, wo man hingehört", bezeichnen.

Der ehemalige Führer des Tūhoe-Stammes, John Rangiāniwaniwa Rangihau, hat die Bedeutung des Marae für sein Volk einmal so erklärt:

„Marae sind unsere Zufluchtsorte,
Stätten, die es uns ermöglichen
mit unserer Lebensart fortzufahren und
an den Begriffen und Werten unserer Kultur festzuhalten.
Wir brauchen den Marae
um in der Kunst des Redens zu wachsen,
um unsere Toten zu beweinen,
um zu unserem Gott zu beten,
um unsere Gäste zu beherbergen,
um unsere Versammlungen durchzuführen,
um unsere Hochzeiten und
unsere Wiedersehen zu feiern,
um zu singen und zu tanzen,
um die Geschichte unseres Volkes zu lernen und um den Reichtum
des Lebens und das stolze Erbe zu verstehen, welches unser ist."

In Neuseeland gibt es etwa achthundert Marae und während meines Aufenthalts hatte ich anlässlich von Trauerfeiern, zeremoniellen Begrüßungen und Hochzeiten viele Gelegenheiten, verschiedene dieser Versammlungsstätten zu besuchen.

Neben dem Versammlungshaus (*whare hui*) befinden sich auf dem Marae-Gelände in der Regel noch ein Speisesaal, ein Schlafsaal, die Toiletten und ein Friedhof. Obwohl der Begriff „Marae" gewöhnlich nur auf den umgrenzten und unbebauten Bereich unmittelbar vor dem Versammlungshaus zutrifft, wird er synonym für das gesamte Areal gebraucht.

Die meisten Stämme, Unterstämme und auch kleineren Māori-Gemeinschaften haben auch heute noch ihren eigenen Marae. Die Menschen, die dem Marae zugehörig sind werden *tangata whenua*, „Menschen des Landes", genannt. Für jeden Marae gilt ein eigenes Protokoll, das von den Gastgebern festgelegt wird und das Verhalten auf dem Marae-Gelände regelt.

So ist es im Versammlungshaus zum Beispiel nicht gestattet, Schuhe zu tragen, zu rauchen, zu essen oder gar die Schnitzereien oder Bilder als Kleiderhaken zu benutzen. Im Speisesaal sollte man davon Abstand nehmen auf den Tischen zu sitzen oder seinen Teller über den Köpfen anderer Gäste hinweg zu balancieren. Durch das Beachten des Protokolls erweist man sowohl den Gastgebern als auch den kulturellen Traditionen der Māori Respekt. Wenn man nicht sicher ist, wie man sich auf dem Marae-Gelände verhalten soll, dann orientiert man sich am besten an dem, was die anderen Anwesenden tun.

as Pōwhiri

Bei formellen Zusammenkünften ist das *pōwhiri*, die traditionelle Begrüßungszeremonie der Māori, der Schlüssel zum Betreten des Marae.

Wann immer man an einem Pōwhiri teilnimmt, wird man von den Gastgebern mit Würde und Respekt willkommen geheißen. Der Begriff *waewae tapu*, „heilige Füße", den die Gastgeber auf ihre Gäste anwenden, bezeichnet treffend die hohe Stellung, die ihnen zuerkannt wird.

Mein erstes Pōwhiri erlebte ich anlässlich des „Carving-Weekend", das an der Kura Kaupapa Schule stattfand. Bevor mit dem Projekt begonnen wurde, veranstalteten die Gastgeber zu Ehren der Gäste ein Pōwhiri.

An diesem Abend hatte ich mich mit vielen anderen Besuchern vor den Toren des Marae eingefunden. Zunächst wurde in einem Gebet (*inoi*) um Führung und Schutz für die Teilnehmer ersucht. Danach stellten wir uns in Zweierreihen vor dem Eingang auf, Frauen und Kinder zuerst, dicht ge-

Pages 60/61: Te Noho Kotahitanga Marae at Unitec's Mt Albert campus in Auckland, North Island

folgt von den Männern.

Das Formieren der Gäste vor dem Eingangstor ist für die Gastgeber das Zeichen mit dem Pōwhiri zu beginnen.

Ein Pōwhiri besteht aus folgenden Elementen:

Karanga	Willkommensruf
Whaikōrero	Rede
Koha	Spende
Hongi	Pressen der Nase
Hākari	Essen

Eingeleitet wurde das Pōwhiri durch den Willkommensruf, den sogenannten *karanga.* Eine der älteren Frauen aus den Reihen der Gastgeber, die vor dem Versammlungshaus stand, erhob ihre Stimme zum Gesang und gleichzeitig setzten wir uns langsam in Bewegung. Bevor die erste Stimme verhallte, erwiderte eine Frau aus unseren Reihen den Ruf. Dieser Wechselgesang, der so durchdringend und intensiv war, dass mir ein Schauder über den Rücken lief, dauerte so lange an, bis wir vor dem Versammlungshaus angekommen waren.

Mit diesem ersten Ruf wird der Marae heilig (tapu). Alle kommenden Elemente des Pōwhiri sind darauf ausgerichtet, diesen einschränkenden Zustand von den Besuchern zu nehmen, so dass sie mit den Gastgebern „eins" werden können.

Die Sitzordnung im Versammlungshaus sah vor, dass die Männer die vorderen Reihen belegten und die Frauen die hinteren. In der darauffolgenden Stunde kam es zu einem verbalen Austausch (*whaikōrero*) zwischen Sprechern aus der Gruppe der Gastgeber und einem Redner aus unserer Gruppe. Dabei wechselten sich beide Gruppen in ihren Reden ab, wobei die Gastgeberseite den Anfang machte.

Das Vorrecht im Marae zu sprechen wird ausschließlich befähigten Rednern zuteil. Beim Whaikōrero stellen die Männer durch das Verwenden von Metaphern und Gleichnissen ihre Sprachgewandtheit und ihre rhetorischen Fähigkeiten unter Beweis.

Als unser Sprecher seine letzte Rede abgeschlossen hatte, platzierte er vor den Gastgebern einen Umschlag, der eine Geldspende (*koha*) enthielt. Der Zweck des Koha besteht darin die Gastgeber im Unterhalt des Marae zu unterstützen sowie die Ausgaben zu decken, die durch die Zusammenkunft (*hui*) entstanden sind. In früheren Zeiten brachten die Gäste das als Koha dar, was in ihrer Heimatregion wertvoll war, z. B. Walknochen, Meeresfrüchte oder aufwendig gewebte Umhänge. Die so dargebrachten Gaben brachten sowohl dem Geber als auch dem Empfänger Ansehen (*mana*) ein.

Nachdem der letzte Redner auf der Gastgeberseite mit seiner Ansprache zu Ende gekommen war, sang dessen Gruppe ein Lied (*waiata*). Durch diesen Gesang wurde das in der Rede gesagte noch einmal bekräftigt und untermauert.

Im Anschluss daran wurden wir ermuntert nach vorne zu kommen und uns mit den Gastgebern bekannt zu machen. Obwohl auch das Händeschütteln (*harirū*) Teil der Begrüßung ist, liegt die größte Bedeutung im *hongi*, dem Pressen von Nase und Stirn. Der Hongi versinnbildlicht den Austausch des Atems des Lebens, ohne den auf dieser Erde keine Existenz möglich ist.

Nach dem Verlassen des Versammlungshauses wurden wir im Speisesaal mit einem gemeinsamen Essen (*hākari*) mit den Gastgebern zusammengeführt. Mit diesem Mahl, das in der Regel aus einem *hāngi* (Essen, das im Erdofen zubereitet wird) besteht, wurde das Begrüßungszeremoniell offiziell beendet. Gleichzeitig wurde der Zustand des Tapu von den Gästen genommen.

Ein Blick in das Whare Hui

Nach dem Essen nutzte ich die Zeit um das Versammlungshaus noch einmal näher zu betrachten. Dabei hatte ich das Vorrecht, jemanden an meiner Seite zu haben, der mir die einzelnen Elemente des für die Māori so wichtigen Gebäudes erklärte.

Auf der nachfolgenden Seite sehen Sie eine Abbildung des Versammlungshauses (*whare hui*) oder „Haus der Vorfahren" (*whare tūpuna*). Wenn man in das Whare Hui hineingeht, dann betritt man nicht etwa ein gewöhnliches Haus sondern man beschreitet ein historisches Geschichtsbuch oder ein lebendiges Archiv.

In seinem Aufbau ist das Whare Hui einem menschlichen Körper nachempfunden. Es symbolisiert den Leib eines Vorfahren, nach dem das Versammlungshaus benannt ist. Das Gebäude ist reichlich mit Schnitzereien verziert und im Inneren hängen Bilder und Photographien aller Ahnen des Stammes.

Sollten Sie, lieber Leser, Neuseeland bereisen und beim Passieren eines Marae den Wunsch verspüren das Gelände zu besuchen, dann scheuen Sie sich nicht, die Māori, die den Marae verwalten, zu kontaktieren.

1, Tekoteko:
Die geschnitzte Figur, die sich auf dem Dach des Versammlungshauses befindet, versinnbildlicht das Haupt des Vorfahren

2, Maihi:
Der Ortgang verkörpert die gestreckten Arme des Vorfahren, die den Gast als Geste des Willkommens umarmen

3, Raparapa:
Die Verlängerung des Ortgangs versinnbildlicht die Finger des Vorfahren

4, Amo:
Die geschnitzte Figur auf den beiden Pfosten symbolisiert die beiden Körperseiten des Vorfahren

5, Tāhuhu:
Bezeichnet die Firststange im Versammlungshaus, die das Rückgrat des Vorfahren repräsentiert

6, Heke:
Die Dachsparren an beiden Seiten der Firststange verkörpern die Rippen des Vorfahren

Wenn man sich als Besucher respektvoll und mit aufrichtigem Interesse ihrer Kultur nähert, sind die Māori gerne bereit, Einzelheiten zu ihrem Marae und seiner Geschichte zu erläutern.

Für mich waren die Besuche auf dem Marae und die damit einhergehenden Pōwhiri eine der schönsten Erfahrungen, die ich während meines Aufenthalts bei den Māori machen durfte.

Die Māori-Küche

Ngā momo Kai a Te Māori

Māori Food

Mate atu he tētē kura, whakaeke mai he tētē kura

A fern frond dies, but another frond rises to take its place

Wann immer ich ins Ausland reise freue mich darauf, dort typische Landesgerichte zu probieren. Daher war ich sehr neugierig auf die Māori-Küche mit ihren Speisen, deren Namen spannend und exotisch klingen und keinen Hinweis darauf liefern, um was es sich dabei handeln könnte.

Die beste Möglichkeit um mich durch das reiche Repertoire an Māori-Gerichten zu kosten, war der Besuch des „Māori Kai*-Festivals", das in der kleinen Hafenstadt Kāwhia stattfand. Auf dem Festival wurde eine Vielzahl von Gerichten angeboten und mir flogen Begriffe wie *toroi*, *piko piko*, *rēwena par*āoa und *kānga wai* um die Ohren.

Da ich mich bei dem Überangebot nicht entscheiden konnte, übernahm mein Gastgeber To-kowhā die Auswahl und orderte kurzerhand ein *hāngi* für mich.

Ein Hāngi ist für die Māori etwa das, was dem Deutschen sein Schnitzel oder dem Schweden sein Köttbullar. Das Wort Hāngi beschreibt das Essen, das im Erdofen gegart wird. Das vorbereite-te Fleisch und Gemüse wird in Gemüseblätter oder in Alufolie eingepackt und in einen Metallkorb gegeben. Der Korb wird in einem Erdloch auf heißen Steinen platziert, mit nassen Säcken abge-deckt und mit Erde zugeschaufelt. Nach drei Stunden wird das Mahl wieder ausgegraben und ser-viert.

Interessanterweise werden beim Fleisch und beim Gemüse keinerlei Gewürze verwendet. Der außergewöhnliche Geschmack entsteht durch die besondere Art der Zubereitung.

Ein Hāngi bereitet man niemals für sich alleine, da man damit eindeutig zu viel Essen produ-ziert. Selbst wenn man ein Gourmand ist, kann man die Portionen nicht bezwingen. Ein Hāngi kommt bei den Māori daher immer dann auf die Speisekarte, wenn eine große Menge an Men-schen zu verkösten ist, wie z. B. bei Hochzeiten oder Trauerfeiern.

Auf Shopping-Tour mit Charles Royal

Alles erinnerte an einen Einkauf im Supermarkt. Die angenehme Verkaufsatmosphäre wurde durch eine dezente Hintergrundmusik verstärkt, die Ware präsentierte sich frisch und geschmack-voll arrangiert und wie es sich heutzutage gehört, hatte der Kunde seine eigene Einkaufstasche mitgebracht. Das einzig Ungewöhnliche an diesem Einkaufsbummel war, dass ich mich nicht in einem Supermarkt befand, sondern mit dem bekannten Māori-Küchenchef Charles Royal mitten im Regenwald Neuseelands.

Vor ein paar Monaten hatte ich eine DVD gesehen, in der Charles durch den Regenwald stapfte, um dort seine „Einkäufe" zu tätigen. Sofort regte sich in mir der Wunsch, diesen Mann auf einen

*Essen

seiner bekannten Food-Trails quer durch den Busch zu begleiten. Zufällig hatte ich kurz darauf in einem Gespräch mit meiner Freundin Leilani erfahren, dass Charles gleich in ihrer Nähe wohnt. Der Kontakt war schnell hergestellt und obwohl Charles mit seinem Unternehmen KINAKI NZ® alle Hände voll zu tun hat, erklärte er sich nach einem kurzen Treffen dazu bereit, mich auf eine seiner täglichen „Einkaufstouren" in den Busch mitzunehmen.

Ein paar Tage später war es dann soweit, Treffpunkt war der Rotomā-See in der Nähe von Rotorua. Kaum dass wir den Regenwald betreten hatten, stürmte Charles davon. Charles kannte jede vorwitzige Wurzel und jede Unebenheit auf dem Weg, während ich aufpassen musste, auf dem feuchten Untergrund nicht ins Rutschen zu geraten. Immer wieder blieb Charles kurz stehen um etwas vom Waldboden aufzuheben oder um einen Trieb von einer Staude zu knicken. Einmal reichte er mir zur Verkostung eine süßlich schmeckende *tawa*-Beere, dann den Stängel eines Baumes, der erfrischend saftig war. Während Charles mich in die essbare Pflanzenwelt Neuseelands einführte, pflückte er im Vorbeigehen allerhand Leckereien, die er zur weiteren Verwendung in seiner großen Tasche verschwinden ließ.

Charles liebte den Busch, daran bestand kein Zweifel. Er selbst konnte sich keinen schöneren und natürlicheren Arbeitsplatz vorstellen. Das Wissen über die native Pflanzenwelt Neuseelands hatte Charles Büchern entnommen oder in Gesprächen mit den alten und erfahrenen Māori erworben. Während unserer Wanderung berichtete Charles von dem im Regenwald wachsenden Weinstock, dessen Äste von den Māori früher zu Körben verarbeitet wurden um damit Langusten zu fangen, von *kawakawa*, einer Pflanze, die der Blutverdünnung dient, und von *piko piko*, einer delikaten Farnspitze, aus der sich ein köstliches Mahl zaubern lässt.

Als wir nach eineinhalb Stunden den Regenwald verließen, war ich überwältigt von dem Reichtum an Speisen, den Neuseelands Natur bietet. Wie schade, dass nur wenige Menschen mit den Kostbarkeiten vertraut sind, die sich im Busch finden lassen. Während man im Supermarkt viel Geld für Gemüse hinlegen muss, ohne zu wissen, welche Qualität man tatsächlich bekommt, steht im Regenwald alles erntefrisch, unbehandelt und kostenfrei zur Verfügung.

Auch mein Abendessen bestand an diesem Abend aus frischen Zutaten, die der Regenwald geliefert hatte, denn am Ende unserer Tour hatte mir Charles ein großes Büschel frischgepflückten Piko Piko in die Hände gelegt.

Wenn Sie jetzt neugierig geworden sind und ein paar typische Māori-Rezepte ausprobieren wollen, dann lade ich Sie auf den folgenden Seiten dazu ein.

Sollten Sie dadurch so richtig auf den Geschmack kommen und Lust auf mehr Māori-Cuisine haben, dann empfehle ich Ihnen das Kochbuch „Cooking with Charles Royal".

Und nun wünsche ich Ihnen guten Appetit!

Next page: Māori chef Charles Royal at his working place: the rain forest, North Island

Mussel Fritter

Parāoa Parai

Brunnenkresse mit Muscheln

Boil up und Mutu Mutu

Parāoa Parai (frittiertes Brot)

Was Sie benötigen:

6 Tassen Mehl
3 Teelöffel Backpulver
1 Prise Salz
Wasser zum Vermengen

Zubereitung:

Geben Sie das Mehl, das Backpulver und das Salz in eine Schüssel.
Fügen Sie das Wasser hinzu und verarbeiten Sie die Zutaten zu einem geschmeidigen Teig.
Lassen Sie den Teig auf einer bemehlten Fläche zugedeckt etwa 20 Minuten ruhen.
Schneiden Sie den Teig in kleine Stücke (Brötchengröße) und rollen Sie ihn auf Fladengröße aus.
Frittieren Sie die Fladen in der Pfanne oder Fritteuse goldgelb.

Tipp:

Servieren Sie das Parāoa Parai mit Ahornsirup oder Marmelade.
Wenn Sie es lieber deftig mögen, können sie die Fladen auch mit Käse oder Schinken belegen.

Mussel Fritter

Was Sie benötigen:

2 Tassen Mehl
2 Eier
2 Teelöffel Backpulver
etwa eine halbe Tasse Milch
Salz, Pfeffer und Kräuter nach Belieben
Green Shell Muscheln, falls nicht erhältlich, können Sie auch Miesmuscheln verwenden.

Zubereitung:

Verquirlen Sie die Eier, fügen Sie die anderen Zutaten hinzu und schmecken Sie den Teig mit Salz, Pfeffer und Kräutern ab.
Kochen Sie die Muscheln ca. vier Minuten in Wasser.
Lassen Sie die Muscheln abkühlen, schneiden Sie sie klein und heben Sie das Muschelfleisch gleichmäßig unter den Teig.
Erhitzen Sie das Öl und setzen Sie mit einem Esslöffel kleine Teighäufchen in die Pfanne. Drücken Sie die Häufchen flach und braten Sie sie von beiden Seiten goldbraun an.

Tipp:

Servieren Sie das Gericht mit frischem Salat.

Boil up und Mutu Mutu

Was Sie für das Boil up benötigen:

Lammkoteletts, Schweineknochen und Kartoffeln
(je 2 Stück pro Person)
Brunnenkresse oder Blattspinat, Salz und Pfeffer

Zubereitung:

Kochen Sie das Fleisch für ca. 2,5 Stunden in Wasser. Fügen Sie die Kartoffeln hinzu und lassen Sie das Ganze für weitere 25 Minuten auf dem Herd köcheln. Würzen Sie das Boil up mit Salz und Pfeffer. Fügen Sie die Brunnenkresse hinzu und kochen Sie alles für weitere 15 Minuten. Achten Sie darauf, dass die Zutaten mit Wasser bedeckt sind. Ein Umrühren ist während des Kochvorgangs nicht erforderlich.

Was Sie für das Mutu Mutu benötigen:

Mehl und Wasser

Zubereitung:

Bereiten Sie aus Mehl und Wasser einen Teig. Formen Sie daraus kleine Bällchen und geben Sie diese in den Topf mit dem Boil-up. Kochen Sie das Ganze weitere 10 Minuten.

Brunnenkresse mit Muscheln

Was Sie benötigen:

Einen großen Büschel Brunnenkresse oder gehackter Spinat
500 g frische Muscheln, bevorzugt Green Shell

Zubereitung:

Reinigen Sie die Brunnenkresse und schneiden Sie sie klein.
Blanchieren Sie die Blätter und kochen Sie sie 10 Minuten in leicht gesalzenem Wasser.
Schneiden Sie die Muscheln in kleine Stücke und geben Sie diese zu der gekochten Brunnenkresse.
Lassen Sie die Masse abkühlen.

Tipp:

Das Gericht schmeckt lecker mit Brot und Butter.

Whenever I am traveling abroad I am always excited to taste the typical local dishes of the country. Therefore I was very curious about the Māori cuisine with all its dishes whose names sounded exotic and exciting along with the mystery of not knowing what I could expect.

The best way to get an idea of the rich repertoire of Māori food was to visit the "Māori Kai* Festival" that was held in the small harbour town of Kāwhia. At the festival a wide range of Māori dishes were offered and I was confronted with terms such as *toroi*, *piko piko*, *rēwena parāoa* and *kānga wai*.

Since I was unable to cope with the decision of what to have my host Tokowhā took over and without further consultation ordered a *hāngi* for me.

The *hāngi* is for the Māori people what the Schnitzel is for the Germans and the Köttbullar for the Swedish. The term *hāngi* describes the Māori food that is cooked in the earth oven. The prepared food, meat and vegetables, are wrapped in green vegetables or alternately tin foil and placed into a metal basket. The basket is placed on top of hot stones that are heated in a hole in the ground. Then the basket is covered with water soaked sacks and shovelled up. After three hours the hāngi is lifted from the hole and the food is served.

Interestingly when preparing the meat and the vegetables for the hāngi no spices are used. The exceptional taste is created by the special way of preparing the food buried under the earth.

A hāngi will never be cooked for just one person, as with a hāngi obviously too much food is produced. Even if the host is a gourmand he will not be able to cope with the portions! Therefore a hāngi is always on the menu if a large crowd of people has to be catered, such as at weddings or funerals.

Shopping with Charles Royal

Everything reminded me of a shopping tour in the supermarket. The pleasant shopping atmosphere was enhanced by discreet background music, the goods were presented in a fresh and tasty way, and as is common today the customer had brought his own shopping bag. The only unusual thing about this shopping trip was that I was not in a supermarket, but with well-known Māori chef Charles Royal in the midst of New Zealand's rain forest.

A few months earlier I had seen Charles on a DVD where he was wandering through the rain forest to do his shopping. Immediately my desire grew to accompany him on one of his famous food trails into the bush. Amazingly, shortly after that I had learned in a conversation with my

*Food

friend Leilani that Charles lives right next to her. The contact was made quickly and although Charles was very busy with this company KINAKI NZ® he agreed to take me on one of his daily "shopping tours".

A few days later early in the morning Charles and I met at Lake Rotomā close to Rotorua. Once we entered the rainforest, Charles took off, while I stumbled after him. Charles knew every cheeky root and every bump on the road while I had to watch out, not to slip and fall on the sloppy ground. Time after time Charles paused for a moment and picked up something from the forest floor or bent a shoot from a bush and handed it to me for tasting, once a sweetish *tawa* berry, and then a stalk which was filled with a refreshing juice. While Charles introduced me to the edible plants of New Zealand he picked all kinds of goodies, which disappeared for future use in his big bag.

Charles loves the bush, there was no doubt about that and he could not imagine a more beautiful and more natural workplace. The knowledge about New Zealand's native flora Charles acquired from books or from conversations with the old and experienced Māori. During our walking tour Charles told me about the long growing vine, whose branches in former times have been processed into baskets to catch crayfish; he also introduced me to *kawakawa*, a plant that is used as blood thinner and to *piko piko*, tasty fiddlehead fern shoots which can be easily prepared into a delicious meal.

When we left the rain forest after an hour, I was overwhelmed by the abundance of food New Zealand's nature offers. What a waste, that only a few people are familiar with the treasures that can be found in the bush. While one has to pay a lot of money for the vegetables in the supermarket without even knowing what kind of quality one actually gets, the vegetables that can be found in the rain forest are freshly harvested, organic and free.

With a smile on my face I started to drive home that night, next to me a large bunch of freshly picked Piko Piko that Charles had handed over to me at the end of our Māori food trail.

If you want to try some typical Māori recipes then get inspired by the following simple but delicious dishes, but if you can't get enough of the Māori cuisine then I recommend you get the cook book "Cooking with Charles Royal".

Mauriora - Bon appétit!

Preparing a Hāngi
Zubereitung des Hāngi

Photo 1:
Burning down the wood and heating up the stones
Ein Feuer wird entzündet in dem die Steine erhitzt werden

Photo 2:
Removing the hot stones and the ashes of the hole
Die heißen Steine und die Asche werden aus dem Loch entfernt

Photo 3:
Placing the hāngi basket on top of the hot stones
Der Hāngi-Korb wird auf den heißen Steinen platziert

Photo 4:
After covering the basket with wet sacks the hāngi basket is covered with soil
Der Korb wird mit nassen Säcken abgedeckt und mit Erde zugeschaufelt

Photo 5:
After three hours the hāngi is removed from the hole and served
Nach drei Stunden wird das Hāngi aus dem Loch geholt und serviert

Parāoa Parai (Fried Bread)

What you need:

2 cups flour
3 teaspoons of baking powder
Pinch of salt
Water to mix

How to prepare:

Put dry ingredients into a bowl.
Pour water and mix to a light dough.
Knead lightly. Place dough on a floured surface, cut into small pieces (scone size).
Heat oil, when hot, place in prepared pieces.
Brown both sides, remove from heat and put on to a tray.

Serving suggestion:

Serve with syrup or jam.

Mussel Fritters

What you need:

2 cups flour
2 eggs
Salt, pepper and herbs
2 tsp baking powder
About half cup milk
Green Shell mussels

How to prepare:

Beat the eggs well and add the other ingredients, mixing until smooth in texture. Throw the mussels into hot boiling water for 2-4 minutes. Slice them into small pieces and add to batter. Fry in spoonful's in hot fat until cooked.

Serving suggestion:

Serve the dish with fresh salad.

Boil up and Mutu Mutu

What you need for the Boil up:

Lamb chops, pork bones and potatoes
(2 per person)
Watercress
Salt and pepper

How to prepare:

Boil meat for 2,5 hours in water, add potatoes and cook for 25 minutes, season with salt and pepper. Add the cleaned watercress and cook for another 15 minutes. Ensure all food is covered with sufficient water. It is not necessary to stir the dish at any stage of cooking.

What you need for the Mutu Mutu:

Wheat flour and water

How to prepare:

Mix flour and water and prepare dough. Make little balls out of it and add them to the boil up. Cook for another 10 minutes.

Watercress with Mussels

What you need:

A bunch of watercress
500 g fresh Green Shell mussels

How to prepare:

Wash watercress thoroughly. Cut up small and blanch with boiling water. Put into boiler and cook for 10 minutes in salted water. Cut mussels into small pieces and mix into the jars of watercress.

Serving suggestion:

This makes a delicious cold dish to have with bread and butter.

$\mathcal{L}$ooking for Kai

I have cancelled my breakfast. When you visit a Food Festival you don't need anything to eat – that's what I thought! If I had thrown a glance at a map I certainly wouldn't have left the house without having a big bowl of muesli.

Our destination is Kāwhia, a small town on the west coast with about 600 inhabitants. Once a year at the traditional Māori Kai Festival, a festivity in which food plays the main role, the number of visitors climbs up to about 10 000.

The road takes us smoothly over the curves of the hillside and all is going well until we reach Tihiroa. We turn onto State Highway 31 and promptly find ourselves in front of an open bonnet. Grey haze is rising from the interior of a pick-up into the sultry air. "Too hot", says the Māori lady and grins a nearly toothless smile. Tirelessly she pours water into the radiator, which bubbles and steams like a geyser. Curious children's eyes examine us from the open side windows.

Tokowhā, my Māori guide, takes a closer look at the engine and shakes his head. With this vehicle the family will definitely not get to Kāwhia today.

After Tokowhā's condemning judgement the smile on the woman's face dies and we all stare accusingly at the engine, which has ruined the family's day. The Māori lady remains at the roadside, waiting for help while we continue our journey.

Tokowhā tries to recoup the lost minutes and drives as fast as the tight corners and his expertise will allow. My stomach responds with a loud growl, but except for a wrinkled old apple which I find in the glove box, there is nothing I can offer it.

By the time we arrive in Kāwhia it is already noon. The streets are packed with cars and at the entrance a long queue has formed. Alcohol and nicotine are taboo on the site. Smokers, who cannot survive the afternoon without a cigarette, have a last smoke before they enter the fray.

Merchants offer wood carvings and jewellery and somewhere far in the distance I catch a sight of colourful sarongs flapping in the wind. My eyes linger only for seconds on the sales tables and get stuck instead on the faces of the visitors; faces so expressive, so individual and stamped by life that I cannot help but ask for permission to take a photo.

I follow Tokowhā who unerringly paves himself a way through the crowd and stops in front of an oversized menu card. The range of Māori kai is so abundant that I am entirely overwhelmed and don't know what to choose. Signs surround me tempting me to try a traditional "Hāngi", "Creamed Paua in Fried Bread," "Mussel Fritters", "Toroi", fermented watercress with mussel meat, "Pan Fried Mussel Kebab", "Piko Piko", fiddlehead fern shoots, "Curry Mussels", "Rēwena Parāoa", bread made with real potato starch, and "Kānga wai".

Kānga wai, also called "Rotten corn", is corn on a cob that has been vegetating in water for months until it eventually ferments. From this kind of preparation you can imagine its scent. Novices are advised to hold their noses until they have placed the kānga wai in their mouth. Apparently it has an extraordinary taste! This is a dish which is mainly liked by the older Māori and originates from the time when food stocks were preserved only by pickling or drying.

Tokowhā cannot bear my indecision any longer and without further ado he orders a hāngi. For a vegetarian this is not necessarily the best choice. However, the search for the perfect kai has exhausted my guide and he stretches out under a tree.

As inconspicuously as possible I rummage about in the little woven basket for the vegetables and the fried bread. While I nibble on a piece of sweet potato I resolve to indulge in the rich selection of desserts later.

The mood is relaxed. The sound of reggae music blends with children's laughter as they leap off the harbour bridge into the sea desperate to cool off.

Visitors wanting to try something new beyond the kai, sun and sea can experiment with flax weaving (*raranga*), wood carving (*whakairo rākau*) and cloak making (*whatu-kākahu*).

As for me, I am still hunting down the perfect kai. As expected I find it in the desserts stall. "Watermelon with vanilla ice cream" and a portion of "Steamed pudding with custard" are just what I have been looking for. The crowd in front of the stand is long, but my desire for the delicacies converts me into a patient person.

When I finally escape the crowd with my favourite kai the sea is busily filling up the swampy puddles which it had left on its departure a few hours earlier.

I make myself comfortable in the shade and after some minutes a flock of seagulls join me. Violent fights break out over the few crumbs that I offer them and within seconds the food has disappeared down their scrawny throats. The birds seem not to be able to rejoice in their food and so as if I wanted to teach a lesson to the greedy diners I sit back and slowly savour every bite of my kai. Yes, life is beautiful, especially when one has found the perfect kai.

Die Sprache

Te Reo

The Language

Ka uia tonutia e koe, ka roa tonu te ara; ka kore koe e uiui, ka poto te ara

The more you ask, the longer the way seems to be; the less you ask, the shorter the journey

$\mathcal{D}$ie Sprache ist ein wichtiger Bestandteil der Kultur eines Volkes und wenn man sich ernsthaft für eine Kultur interessiert, dann möchte man zumeist auch deren Sprache sprechen - oder es zumindest versuchen. Da sich meine Māori-Kenntnisse auf *Kia ora*, was mit „Hallo" oder „Danke" übersetzt werden kann, beschränkten, beschloss ich mich in Neuseeland mit der Māori-Sprache vertraut zu machen.

$\mathcal{W}$ie funktioniert Māori?

Die Sprache erreichte Neuseeland etwa im Jahr 1100, als die ersten polynesischen Einwanderer ihr Kanu an Land zogen. Die frühen Māori verfügten allerdings über keine geschriebene Sprache. Wissen, das bewahrt werden sollte, wurde in Schnitzereien, Webearbeiten oder Liedern festgehalten und so von einer Generation an die andere weitergegeben.

Im Jahr 1814 unternahmen eingewanderte Missionare die ersten Versuche, die Māori-Sprache niederzuschreiben. Die Möglichkeit, das Schreiben und Lesen zu erlernen, wurde von den Māori begeistert aufgenommen und bereits einige Jahre später berichteten die Missionare davon, wie Māori sich gegenseitig in diesen Fertigkeiten unterrichteten.

Im Māori-Alphabet werden, wie in der deutschen Sprache, fünf Vokale verwendet. Die Aussprache erfolgt wie im Deutschen:

a, e, i, o, u

Da der Unterschied zwischen langen und kurzen Vokalen oft eine andere Bedeutung des Wortes zur Folge hat, werden die langen Vokale durch ein Makron, einen waagrechten Strich über dem Buchstaben, gekennzeichnet:

ā, ē, ī, ō, ū

Bei den Konsonanten gibt es acht einfache Buchstaben:

h, k, m, n, p, r, t, w

und zwei zusammengesetzte, sogenannte Digraphen:

ng und **wh**,

ng wird wie in dem Wort „An**g**el" ausgesprochen und **wh** wie das „**f**" in dem Wort „**F**isch".

Zu erwähnen sind noch die Diphthonge, bei denen es in der Māori-Sprache mehr gibt als im Deutschen:

ae, ai, ao, au, oi, ou, oe

Beide Selbstlaute werden aneinandergehängt und nacheinander vollständig ausgesprochen.

Interessant ist Māori vor allem wegen der häufigen Benutzung des Passivs. Sagen wir im Deutschen: „Ich habe die Kartoffel gegessen", so würde die wortgetreue Übersetzung des Māori-Satzes lauten: „Wurde von mir gegessen die Kartoffel."

Ein Volk ohne Sprache

Als ich nach Neuseeland kam, hegte ich keinen Zweifel daran, dass die meisten in Aotearoa lebenden Māori ihrer Sprache mächtig sind und es mir somit problemlos gelingen würde, einen passenden Lehrer zu finden. Zu meiner Überraschung beherrschten jedoch nur ganz wenige der Māori mit denen ich Kontakt hatte, die Sprache gut genug, um sie an andere weitergeben zu können. Doch was ist der Grund für diese Situation?

Zu Beginn des neunzehnten Jahrhunderts war Māori die vorherrschende Sprache in Aotearoa und selbst für Regierungsbeamte aus den Reihen der Pākehā war es damals nicht ungewöhnlich, Māori zu sprechen. Eine weitere Gruppe, die die Māori-Sprache beherrschte, waren die Missionare, die eifrig darum bemüht waren, den Einheimischen ihre Glaubensansichten zu vermitteln.

Doch als sich in den frühen 1860er Jahren der Anteil an Europäern vergrößerte, kam es zu einer Wende. Zu jener Zeit betrachtete kaum einer die Māori-Sprache als wesentliches Element der Māori-Kultur. In einer von den Europäern dominierten Welt bezweifelten selbst viele Māori die Relevanz ihrer Sprache. Englisch wurde als "bread-and-butter language" angesehen, als die Sprache, die die Familie ernährte. *Kōrero Pākehā*, „Sprich Englisch", war die Devise unter der Māori-

Bevölkerung, weshalb viele Eltern ihre Kinder ermunterten Englisch zu lernen. Im Jahr 1867 wurde im Native Schools Act per Gesetz angeordnet, dass bei der Erziehung der Māori-Kinder ausschließlich die englische Sprache verwendet werden sollte. Durch diese Anweisung kam es schließlich dazu, dass das Sprechen von Māori an den Schulen verboten wurde.

Der Zweite Weltkrieg brachte für die Māori und ihre Sprache weitere massive Veränderungen mit sich. Da Arbeit zumeist nur in den Städten zu finden war, mussten die Māori ihre Heimat und damit auch einen Teil ihrer Kultur hinter sich lassen. Viele kehrten nur mehr in ihre Dörfer zurück, wenn es galt an Hochzeiten oder Beerdigungen teilzunehmen. Lebten vor dem Krieg etwa fünfundzwanzig Prozent der Māori-Bevölkerung in städtischen Zentren, waren es zwei Jahrzehnte später etwa sechzig Prozent.

Die Auswirkungen auf das Sprachverhalten ließen nicht lange auf sich warten. Englisch war allgegenwärtig, ob im Beruf, in der Schule oder in der Freizeit. Mit der Zeit nahm die Anzahl der Māori sprechenden Personen daher rapide ab. In den 80er Jahren waren nur mehr etwa zwanzig Prozent der Māori in der Lage, sich fließend in ihrer Sprache zu unterhalten.

Mōkai Native School in den 1930er Jahren
Mōkai Native School in the 1930's

Eine Zeit der Wiederbelebung

Nach vielen Jahrzehnten der Veränderungen und Anpassungen machten sich in den 1970er Jahren viele Māori auf die Suche nach ihrer Identität und ihren Wurzeln. Damit rückte auch die Māori-Sprache wieder in den Fokus. Nach all den Jahren, in denen der Erhalt der Sprache vernachlässigt worden war, wurde jetzt deutlich, dass Māori im Aussterben begriffen war.

Um dem entgegen zu wirken wurden von Seiten der Māori immense Anstrengungen unternommen, die Sprache zu revitalisieren. Man begann damit bilinguale Schulen einzurichten, in denen Englisch und Māori unterrichtet wurde. Zur Früherziehung wurden sogenannte *Kōhanga Reo*, „Māori-Sprachnester", gegründet, in denen die Kinder an die Sprache ihres Volkes herangeführt und ihnen die Bräuche (*tikanga*) ihrer Vorfahren vermittelt wurden. Im Jahr 1983 ging das Māori-Radioprogramm *Te Reo-o-Pōneke* auf Sendung, zehn Jahre später folgte der Fernsehsender *Māori Television*. All diese Maßnahmen trugen dazu bei, die Māori-Sprache wieder lebendig werden zu lassen. Den größten Erfolg für die Erhaltung ihrer Sprache erzielten die Māori im Jahr 1987, als Māori als eine offizielle Sprache Neuseelands anerkannt wurde.

In den letzten Jahrzehnten hat Māori zwar wieder an Bedeutung gewonnen, doch in einer stark von europäischen Einflüssen geformten Gesellschaft ist die Māori-Sprache noch immer zerbrechlich und schutzbedürftig. Das Recht, sich in seiner Sprache auszudrücken, ist das unschätzbare Gut der individuellen Freiheit des Einzelnen. Jede Sprache, die auf dieser Erde gesprochen wird, ist das kostbare Vermögen eines Volkes und stellt das Band dar, das uns mit unserer menschlichen Geschichte verbindet.

"Ko taku Reo taku Māpihi Mauria"

"Meine Sprache ist das Fenster zu meiner Seele"

Sprichwort der Māori

*L*anguage is an important part of the culture of a people and if one is seriously interested in a culture, then he usually wants to speak their language - or at least try. Except for *Kia ora*, which can be translated as "Hello" and "Thank you", I didn't know any other Māori words and therefore decided to get more familiar with the Māori language, while I was in New Zealand.

*H*ow the Māori language works

The language came to New Zealand around the year 1100 when the Polynesian immigrants pulled their canoes to the shore. The early Māori had no formal written language. To pass knowledge on to the next generation, Māori people used carvings, weaving or songs.

Around 1814 missionaries made first attempts to write down the Māori language. The ability to write and read was accepted enthusiastically by the Māori and a few years later missionaries reported how Māori taught each other these skills.

In the Māori alphabet, as with the German language, there are five vowels which are pronounced as the German vowels:

a, e, i, o, u

There are long and short vowels. The long vowels are marked by a macron, a bar appearing over the vowel:

ā, ē, ī, ō, ū

There are eight single consonants:

h, k, m, n, p, r, t, w

and two composite consonants, called digraphs:

ng and **wh**

ng is said as in the word "si**ng**er" and **wh** is pronounced as the English **"f"**.

There are also diphthongs, like:

ae, ai, ao, au, oi, ou, oe

Both vowels are linked together whereby each vowel is fully pronounced.

An interesting thing about the Māori language is the frequent use of the passive construction. Would we say in English "I have eaten the potato", the Māori translation would be: *Kua kainga e au te rīwai,* that literally means "Has been eaten by me the potato".

$\mathcal{P}$eople without a Language

When I arrived in New Zealand I had no doubt that most of the Māori people living in Aotearoa were fluent in their language and that consequently it would not be difficult to find a suitable Māori teacher. I was quite surprised to find out that only a few Māori I knew were able to speak the Māori language in a way to share it with others. You may with reason ask 'why'?

At the beginning of the 19th century Māori was the predominant language spoken in Aotearoa and even for government officials who were Pākehā it was not unusual to speak Māori. Another group that mastered the Māori language was the missionaries who were eagerly trying to convert Māori of their religious beliefs.

As the population rate of the Europeans in New Zealand increased, the situation changed. At this time the Māori language was not considered as a valued element in connection with the culture. In a world dominated by the Pākehā, many Māori themselves questioned the relevance of the Māori language. English was viewed as the "bread-and-butter language", the instrument to feed the family. *Kōrero Pākehā*, "Speak English", was the motto and many Māori parents encouraged their children to learn English. With the Native Schools Act, that was installed in 1867 it was written by law that in the education of Māori children the English language would be exclusive. With this statement it was not surprising that shortly after Māori was declared a forbidden language in New Zealand schools.

The Second World War brought momentous changes for the Māori society. The cities offered many job opportunities and therefore many Māori left their homes and a part of their culture behind. Before the war, about 25% of the Māori lived in urban areas, two decades later it increased to approximately 60%.

The impact on the language was soon to come. English was omnipresent, it was essential at work, at school and in recreation. Over time the number of people speaking Māori declined. In the 1980's only 20% of the Māori people were able to speak the language fluently.

𝒜 Time of Revitalization

In the 1970s after many centuries of changes and adjustments many Māori started to search for their identity. With that development the value of the Māori language increased. Although Māori who were fluent in the language advocated for retention and development, Māori language was on the wane. Māori leaders were aware of the threat that would arise with the loss of the language. During the 1980s big efforts have been made to revitalise Te reo Māori.

Bilingual schools were founded, where English and Māori were taught. In the early education sector so called *Kōhanga Reo*, "Māori-language nests", were established with the goal of familiarising children with the Māori language and the customs (*tikanga*) of their ancestors. In 1983 the first Māori-owned radio station *Te Reo-o-Pōneke went* on air. Ten years later the television channel *Māori Television* followed. All these efforts had a role in bringing Te reo Māori back to life and to integrate it into daily life. The greatest success and land mark legislation for the preservation of the Māori language was achieved in 1987, when Māori was recognised as an official language of New Zealand.

Although Māori has regained a marginal position of importance in the recent decades, in a society heavily shaped by European influences, Māori language is still fragile and vulnerable.

The right to speak in our language is an invaluable asset of individual freedom. Every language that is spoken on this earth is the precious wealth of a nation and represents the bond that connects us to our history.

"Ko taku Reo taku Māpihi Mauria"

"My language is the window to my soul"

Māori proverb

Kurzbiographien

He Kōrero a Tangata kē

Profiles

Waiho mā te tangata e mihi
Let someone else acknowledge your virtues

Pipiana Hetet

Pepeha

Ko Tainui te waka

Ko Ngāti Raukawa te Iwi

Ko Tītīraupenga te maunga

Ko Waikato taku awa

Ko Pakaketaiari te tūpuna whare

Nō Mōkai ahau

Ko Pipiana Hetet (Ko Rangikataua hoki) tōku ingoa

Tēnā tātou katoa

"Nō te 8 o Hōngongoi, kotahi mano, iwa rau, toru tekau mā whā i whānau tonu mai au ki Mōkai. Ko au te tamaiti tuangahuru o ōku mātua. Tokomaha ngā pēpi Māori i whānau whānuitia mai ana ki te kainga i taua wā. I reira kē atu hoki tētehi whanaunga matatau ki te manaaki pēpi. I whānau mai au i te rā i mate tūturu ko tōku kuia, ko Pipiana Rangikataua te ingoa ā i rēhitatia tōku ingoa ki tōna ake, ko Pipiana Rangikataua.

Nō te rima tau au e haere atu ana ki te Kura Māori tūturu o Mōkai. I te rā tuatahi i whakahuria tōku ingoa e ngā māhita nō tō rātou kaha koretake ki te whakahua ingoa Māori, ka huri ki "Anna Rangi" kē. Nō rātou hoki te whakaaro kuare whakahīhī, he mea kore noa iho me tāku hoki nō tōku moroiti kōpuapua nohinohi. Ki muri ake au ka mārama, he mea tino whakahirahira tōku ingoa me te mea takahi mana tangata nō rātou. Kāore hoki he rongoa i kitea nei e au i taua wā.

I te tau tahi mano, iwa rau ono tekau tau ka whakahokia tōku ingoa tūtuturu ki 'Pipiana Rangikataua'. Ngau mamae aroha taku ingo hotuhotu! Taukiri te reka, te kite atu ki taku ingoa i runga tīwhikete whānau nō muri iho i te rua tekau tau!

Ehara i te mea, ko tēnei nahe te hara kīkino, i wepua tātua kau ki te tamariki mena i kōrerotia ai rātou te reo Māori i rō kura. I pōhēhē hoki ōku mātua, mā te whakakore reo Māori mātou rātou e ārai i te mau patu tamariki. Ko te utu, ko taku reo Māori i te ngaro me taku auetanga atu.

Nō muri mai ka kai mamae kino i te mea, kua ngaro te wairua o taku reo ki āku tamariki mokopuna. Koia rā hoki te kaupapa i haere ai au ki te ako i te reo Māori. Ko te tau iwa rau, iwa tekau mā whā, ono tekau tau kē tōku pakeke i taua wā. Tūmeke!

I te tau rua mano i uru ahau ki Te Wānanga o Aotearoa i Te Kuiti ki te ako raranga. Tae noa mai ki naia tonu nei, e rima ngā korowai i oti pai i a au.

E tino mōhio ana au te mamae o te ngākau ki te mahi whakaparahako o tō tātou reo me ngā tikanga, he parahako tauiwi kē. He mea nunui rawa atu ki a au taku whainga reo Māori, tikanga Māori o Ngai Tāua, hei tikitiki mo te māhunga, me taku mōhio, he Māori ahau, he iwi anō hoki tātou, he iwi toto rangatira."

Pipiana Hetet

Pepeha

My canoe is Tainui

Ngāti Raukawa is my tribe

My mountain is Tītīraupenga

My river is Waikato

Pakaketaiari is my ancestral meeting house

Mōkai is where I come from

Pipiana Hetet, nee Rangikataua, is my name

❧

"I was born at home in Mōkai, New Zealand, on the 8th of July 1934 as the 10th child of my parents. Home births were common amongst Māori during that time. The birth was attended by a family member who was experienced in delivering babies. I was born the same day my great grandmother Pipiana died and was registered Pipiana Rangikataua.

When I was five years old I attended Mōkai Native School. On my first day at school my name was changed to "Anna Rangi" as the teachers said the name is easier to pronounce. For the teachers changing my name was an act of convenience and at the age of five, I didn't understand the significance of that incident. Later in my life I realised that the change of my name was equivalent to the loss of my identity. I knew that I lived under a false name but I didn't know how to reverse it. In the year 1960 the opportunity came along to take my birth name back. It was a very touching moment when I saw my real name Pipiana Rangikataua on my birth certificate after almost twenty years.

But it was not only that my name was changed when I was a child. At school it was also forbidden to speak Māori and pupils who spoke the language were punished with a leather strap. My parents protected me and my siblings from this cruel kind of treatment by not speaking to us in Māori at all. The result was that we didn't learn the language.

Over the years I realised that there was something important missing in my life. Not just that I couldn't speak the language I was also not able to pass it on to my children and grandchildren. For that reason in 1994, at the age of 60, I started attending Māori classes. In 2000 I enrolled in raranga, weaving, in Te Kuiti Te Wananga o Aotearoa and meanwhile I have completed five korowai (Māori cloaks).

I know that there is no way to compensate for the lost years in which our culture was treated as not worthy to be preserved but I am very proud that over the last decades I managed to recover parts of my culture and with this the appreciation of being Māori."

Pipiana Hetet

Pepeha

Mein Kanu ist Tainui

Mein Stamm ist Ngāti Raukawa

Mein Berg ist Tītīraupenga

Mein Fluss ist Waikato

Pakaketaiari ist das Haus meiner Vorfahren

Ich komme aus Mōkai

Pipiana Hetet, geborene Rangikataua, ist mein Name

Grüße an uns alle

✜

„Am 08. Juli 1934 wurde ich als zehntes Kind in Mōkai, Neuseeland, geboren. Hausgeburten waren damals unter Māori üblich und das Ereignis wurde von einem erfahrenen Familienmitglied begleitet.

Im Alter von fünf Jahren besuchte ich die Mōkai Native School und bereits an meinem ersten Schultag wurde mein Name von Pipiana Rangikataua in Anna Rangi abgeändert. Die Lehrer begründeten diese Maßnahme damit, dass der Name leichter auszusprechen sei. Als Fünfjährige nahm ich diese Entscheidung einfach hin. Erst einige Jahre später wurde mir klar, dass diese Namensänderung gleichbedeutend war mit dem Verlust meiner Identität. Obwohl mir bewusst war, dass ich unter einem falschen Namen lebte, sah ich keine Möglichkeit, diesen Zustand zu ändern. Im Jahr 1960 bot sich anlässlich meiner Heirat die Gelegenheit, meinen Geburtsnamen wieder anzunehmen. Es war ein sehr bewegender Moment für mich, nach über zwanzig Jahren meinen wirklichen Namen Pipiana Rangikataua auf der Geburtsurkunde zu sehen.

Doch als Kind war nicht nur mein Name geändert worden, an der Schule war es auch verboten, Māori zu sprechen. Schüler, die es wagten etwas in Māori zu sagen, wurden mit einem Ledergürtel misshandelt. Um meinen Geschwistern und mir diese grausame Behandlung zu ersparen, sprachen meine Eltern in unserem Beisein überhaupt kein Māori. Das hatte allerdings zur Folge, dass wir die Sprache unseres Volkes nicht lernten. Mit der Zeit realisierte ich, dass damit etwas Wichtiges in meinem Leben fehlte. 1994, im Alter von 60 Jahren, belegte ich daher einen Sprachkurs in Māori. Im Jahr 2000 erlernte ich Raranga, das Weben, an der Schule Te Wananga o Aotearoa in Te Kuiti, und mittlerweile habe ich fünf Korowai, Māori-Umhänge, fertig gestellt.

Ich weiß, dass es keine Möglichkeit gibt die verlorenen Jahre wiedergutzumachen, in denen die Māori-Kultur als nicht wertvoll genug erachtet wurde um bewahrt zu werden. Doch ich bin stolz darauf, dass es mir in der Vergangenheit gelungen ist, Teile meiner Kultur zurückzugewinnen und damit die Wertschätzung dafür, eine Māori zu sein.“

Ūekaha Tāne Tinorau

Pepeha

Ko Tainui te waka

Ko Waitomo te awa

Ko Ōwhawhe te maunga

Ko Tokikapu te marae

Ko Ngāti Ūekaha te hapū

Ko Hoturoa te Tangata

Ko Wahanui rāua ko Inuwai ōku mātua

Ko Ūekaha tōku ingoa

☙❦☙

"I whānau ai au i tōku kainga ki Kinohaku, he wāhi tino mokemoke tata ki te wahapū o Kāwhia moana. Nā tōku pāpā ko Claude Wahanui au i whakaputa, ko au te tamaiti tekau mā whā. Mehemea, ka ora tonu mātou katoa, ka tekau mā waru kē.

I whānau hākona kore "kiri kahurangi" ahau, heoi anō, he uaua hoki taku ōranga ki te tekau mā rima tau. I roa te wā, i pāngia ahau e te 'tuberculosis' me ētehi atu momo mate ōranga tamariki ara noa atu taku nohonga ki rō hōhipera. Nā tērā, i te tau 1952 i whakaaetia e ōku mātua te haere ki Waitomo noho 'hāpori tangata' ai. I hangaia tō mātou whare e tōku Pāpā, e rite ki te whare motokā e rua noa iho tana rahi, he mā te tae, e rite ki te 'Pouaka hōtoke makariri', kei raro puke, kei waenganui rākau 'paramū' hoki tō mātou whare pakukū.

He tipuranga tino whakamā ki a au tōku whare 'taretare'. Taukiri te puna mamae aroha te maumāharatia ai. Ataahua ake anō te kupu i whakaahuatia ki a mātou, he kupu ngau aroha atu, tihei te ingoa rangatira ake, ko 'stoonk'! Aue te rite o tana haunga me te pūtake o taua ingoa, he whakapapa pīhau tāna nō tuawhakarere iho.

Nō te kore hikohiko, mai rā anō te pātaka kai Māori, me te tohungatanga ō ōku mātua ki te whakapai kai. Ko te nehu whakauenuku huhua tētehi, ko te rukuwai pēke huka tētehi, ko te whakairirangi kia pāwheratia ai tētehi, kia whakaoti ai, ka whakapounmutia pirautia ai e rite ki te pihau kina e pāterotero mai ana te reka.

Engari, Māori mā, kia mau! E te tino kino o te ataahua o taku whakamā, āe te kīnaki, āe te reka, āe te haunga whakamate pūru tukituki. Tēnā taihoa, ahakoa te kore pōwhiri, e kare, haere kuare tonu mai ōku hoa Pākehā ki te kainga. Heoi atu, kaua rawa e māharatia ai, ka tau poto, ka rongo, ka rere.

Tau ai te taru kino, te mahi whaiāipo tamariki kē, i whakamaugia ahau e te hīnaki a tau o tētehi kohine tauiwi kē, aue te mamae aroha ki tēnei pirinihi. Papa te whatitiri, hikohiko te uira ka horo ngā tihi maunga, ka haruru te whenua! Tau kē, ko tōna pāpā te tumuaki o tō mātou kura. Īnā hoki tētehi pō Māori, kai kānga wai, kai pīhau kina ai, ko wai rā, ko wai rā i whakatau, taukiri taku pirinihi rāua tahi ko tōna pāpā. I whakataungia ahuru Māori rāua e tōku whāea kia kai ai. E kare mā, ka tūpāpaku haere noa atu taku whakamā ki te huna, engari, he kauta pouaka hāwhe hēki, pouaka kurī kē tō mātou, kore kore rawatia ahau i te whai wāhi huna.

He pō mutunga kore, me te mātāpuna o taku rangirua, kia tū tangata ai. Ko wai au? He ao kē tō te Māori, taku tipuranga ake i taua wā he mea nanawe. Taku tirohanga atu, ki tō te iwi Pākehā, te pāmu hirahira, te whare hirahira, te motokā hirahira, te aha, te aha.

Hoki tonu mai ki a ngai tāua te Māori, he tarutaru 'ragwort', he tarutaru 'gorse', he tarutaru 'blackberry' e te katoa ki tō mātou whenua. Tō mātou motokā, te mea koroua, kuia haere, ko 'Konti-lele' te ingoa ataahua. Aua hoki te pūtake o taua ingoa ake. He whare tino 'stoonk' tō mātou, he whāriki pēke huka hoki tō mātou papa kauta i whārikihia. Ara rā te wharepaku ki raro puke, mau pakitara pakukū, pakukū mata pū, engari atu, he pakiwaitara kē atu tēnā.

He rau te huringa tau, huringa wā i hipa, ka tau marie ake te ekenga tapuwae ki tōku taumata, āta whakaarohia ai ki ngā taonga i tuku iho ai. Ao ake ana te takaroa, te pakeke haere o ngā tirohanga whakamuri hei whakaaro matua, aue te aroha ki taku tipuranga, he taonga rangatira.

Kua eke ki tua aua taonga iti kahurangi rehurerhu waharua kōpito, he moemoeā tamariki kau noa tana kohu pūmau pakeke tonu nei. He waka huia. Tāe noa ki ēnei rā, hei kete wānanga i ngā rā o tōku ao. Ko wai atu ahau?, ko Ngāti Ūekaha e tū nei, e mihi nei, e tangi nei, tihei mauri ora!"

Daniel Ormsby

Pepeha

Ko Tainui te waka
Ko Ngāāti Maniapoto te iwi
Ko Pirongia te maunga
Ko Waipaa te awa
Ko Kaputuhi te tupuna whare
Noo Ōtorohanga ahau
Ko Daniel Ormsby tooku ingoa

"Ko taku hiringa matua ko te mahi toi, ko te toi Maaori, aa, naa roto i oona tikanga kua kitea noatia e au he whaainga otiraa he tuuranga hoki mooku ake i te ao nei.

Ki a au nei, ko te waihanga whakairo he mea nui kee, ehara raa i te umanga noa iho; engari he kohara, he rangatiratanga, he ngaakau nui, he koronga. He oranga ngaakau, he pikinga wairua hoki teenei mea te mahi toi, aa, kua puukengatia au e te mahi toi kia maahorahora otira kia whaia e au i te iti kahurangi e ngaakaunuitia ana e au.

He kawenga aa iwi kei roto i te mahi toi. I ngaa raa o mua naa te tohunga whakairo i whakauenuku i te taahuuhuu koorero, i te whakapapa, i ngaa aahutanga wairua i whakaponohia ai e te iwi. Kei mua tonu i aku whakaaro teenei aahuatanga, aa, e matatau ana ahau ki ngaa tikanga, ngaa taonga tuku iho e whakaaturia atu nei e au i te waa e whakairo ana, i te waa e whakaatu ana hoki i ngaa mahi toi nei. Kaatahi raa, kaatahi raa te toi taa moko, he nui kee atu toona awe, toonaa kawekawe ki te hirikapo teera ki te kiri e werohia nei e te uhi. Ko te mutunga iho, e ngana nei ahau kia tino pai aku mahi toi, araa ake anoo ko te toi 'haakoakoa'. Ko te mea he tohungataa Maaori ahau, ko aaku whakatutukitanga ka pakuu atu ki ooku whaanau, ki aaku tamariki, ki te iwi me ooku haapori hoki. Ko haakoatanga e takea mai i taku mahi toi nei he mea whakanui i taaku kaha whakaputa i te wairua ngaakau rorotu ki te tangata ka piri mai ki ahau.

Nooku te koronga kia ora tonu taku mahi toi, aa, kia noho tonu taua mahi raa hei takawaenga i onamata mohoa noa nei ki naianei rangi, aa, maa konei ka whakaputaina atu ki tua hei piki kotuku moo ngaa raa kei te tuu mai."

Translation by Shane Te Ruki

Daniel Ormsby

Pepeha

My canoe is Tainui

Ngāti Maniapoto is my tribe

My mountain is Pirongia

My river is Waipā

Kaputuhi is my ancestral meeting house

Ōtorohanga is where I come from

Daniel Ormsby is my name

"Art is my passion, especially Māori art and it is through this tradition I have found my place and purpose in the world.

For me creating artwork is not just a profession it is passion, freedom, dedication and aspiration. Art satisfies me in both a physical and a spiritual sense and has taught me to keep an open mind and to forever strive.

Māori art entails social responsibilities. Traditionally the carver's role was to record and preserve tribal history, whakapapa and religious or spiritual beliefs. This role is always at the forefront of my mind and I am always aware of the culture and heritage I represent when I produce and display my art. This is especially so with the art of Tā moko where the process of adorning the skin can have a huge influence on the psyche of the recipient.

Ultimately, I endeavour to do my best, especially in the art of "being happy". As a Māori artist, my achievements also become those of my families, my children, my tribe and my cultures. The happiness my passion gives me enhances my capacity to pass positivity on to those around me.

My aspirations with my art is to continue passing on and being a link between the past and the present and project this into the future leaving the legacy that I have inherited as rich as when I picked it up."

Ūekaha Tāne Tinorau

Pepeha

My canoe is Tainui

My river, Waitomo

My mountain is Ōwhawhe

Tokikapu is my marae

My people are Ngāti Ūekaha

My ancestor is Hoturoa

Wahanui and Inuwai are my parents

My name is Ūekaha

"I was born at home in Kinohaku, a very remote place by an inlet harbour near Kāwhia. I was 'number 14' to be delivered by my dad, Claude Wahanui. If we were all alive today there would be eighteen of us.

I was a 'blue baby'. The first fifteen years of my life were a struggle to stay alive. Tuberculosis and other health complications kept me hospitalised for long periods during those times. Because of that, in 1952 our parents decided we should move to Waitomo Caves to be near civilization.

Dad built our whare (house). It was no bigger than a double garage. Painted white it looked like a chilly bin. Our 'Outhouse' was way down the hill among the plum trees. Growing up at my kainga (home) was often a source of embarrassment for me. A word we used then was 'stoonk'. Which loosely means 'a stink house' and literally it was.

Having no electricity meant that my parents used the old traditional ways to preserve food. We either buried it in the ground, put it in a bag in trickling water, hung it up to dry or bottled it (like kina – sea urchins). Hence the taste of these foods was delectable and at times exquisitely delectable. The smell was - well to put a positive spin on it 'highly organic'. These smells seemed to always permeate in and around our kainga.

I can't remember ever inviting my Pākehā mates back to the kainga. If they happened to arrive there by chance it seemed they didn't stay long. When I was 13 I had an enormous crush on this flash Pākehā girl whose father was our headmaster at our school. One night we were having a feed of kānga-wai (fermented corn) and bottled kina-the most 'stink as' kai, and who should visit us? Āe, my dream princess and her teacher dad. What's more, mum invited them in for kai! I mean, the kitchen was the size of ½ dozen dog boxes, where can you hide? I 'died' of shame that night. At that time I developed an identity crisis.

Being Māori didn't feel nice, because of certain circumstances around me, growing up at the time. I observed that the predominantly Pākehā iwi had flash farms, flash houses, flash cars, etc. We on the other hand, had ragwort, gorse, and blackberry on our land. We had an old beat up SX car called Konti-lele (I don't know where the name came from). We lived in a 'stoonk' whare with sugar bags for carpet, and we had an aromatic toilet down the hill with some bullet holes in it. That's another story.

Many years, many seasons have passed by now and often one's life journey brings its own rewards – the ability to truly reflect with humility and humbleness comes with time. I feel blessed now and enriched by my upbringing. Those many moments of bygone years are now treasures stored away in the Wakahuia (Treasure chest) of my head and heart. Those moments are what shaped my life and are still on-going today."

Leilani Rickard

Pepeha

Ko Te Arawa Toku waka tupuna o nehe ra

Ko Te Arawa Toku iwi

Ko Te Arawa toku rohe whenua; Mai l Maketu ki Tongariro

Ko Ngāti Whakaue, ratou ko, Ngāti Rangiwewehi ko Ngāti Rangitihi, ko Ngāti Pikiao

ko Tuhourangi oku hapu matua o taua iwi whanui

No reira

Ko Matawhara toku maunga, ko tera te kohatu korero a pikiao

Ko Te Rotoiti kitea ihenga toku moana piataata

Ko Te Kaituna toku awa kahakaha e rere ana kite moana

Ko Hohowai toku Turangawaewae tuturu

Ko Te Takinga toku tupuna matua e tu ai, e tu ai,e tu ai....

Ko Leilani Grant Rickard toku ingoa

Tihei mauriora!

⤬

"Nō te toru tekau tau taku ao ki te mahi raranga, ehara kē te rā e taka ana i te raranga kore, raranga harakeke, raranga aha. I te rua tau ki mua, i hangaia kākahu hangahanga, kākahu tangata toi whakaari mō te wiki kākahu hirahira o Aotearoa whānui. Tata tonu atu ki muri, ka whiriwhiria ētehi ahowai kākahu muramura tae āniwaniwa hei kākahu hangahanga, ahakoa te kaupapa, atu i te kākahu kapa haka noa iho.

Inā hoki te rerenga tau, he rau te mahi hangahanga piupiu ki te rōpu kapa haka. I taku mahi hanga ahowai tukutuku tāniko, ka whakaaro noa atu, me pēwhea rā te mahi a ngā tūpuna ki ngā tini momo aho raranga o naianei? Ko te tino taonga ki a au o taku mahi, ko tērā te puna whakaaro, kia hanga mai i te ahowai hou, hei mea whakahirahira, hei mea ārai kore ki taku mahi waihanga kaitoi.

Nā taku timatanga mahi hei Kairaranga, i whakaaro ake ka piripono ki te ara akoranga rangatira mai rā anō a ōku pūkenga wai, engari, ka mārama ake ki muri, tāea hoki te pēwhea, ka tūhono tonu ki taku Māoritanga ahakoa taku ekenga tapuwae toiwhakaari ki whea."

Leilani Rickard

Pepeha

Te Arawa is my ancestral waka of days past

My people are Te Arawa

Te Arawa is my land that stretches from Maketu to Mount Tongariro

Matawharua is my lofty mountain for that is the rock of which Pikiao speaks

The small lake discovered by ihenga is my shimmering expanse of water

The Kaituna is my turbulent river that flows to the sea at Maketu

Hohowai is my rightful marae to which i affiliate

Te Takinga is my ancestral house, let him remain always

Leilani Rickard/Grant is my name

Let life energy prevail!

"Weaving has been a part of my life for the last thirty years and very rarely does a day go by where I'm not working with harakeke or fibre. A couple of years ago I made some garments for the fashion show "Wearable Art" and after that I was asked to create six dresses for "NZ Fashion Week". Shortly after that I decided to continue to create more of these challenging pieces of art fashion and so I started to experiment with these vibrant coloured kākahu that can be worn for any occasion and not just for kapa haka.

Over the years I have made hundreds of piupiu for kapa haka groups. In the process of developing new patterns and styles I am inspired by thinking about how our ancestors might have used the different materials. What I really like about my work is the possibility to create something new and extraordinary as there are no set boundaries applying to my work as an artist.

When I started weaving I thought it might be appropriate to follow the path already set by the weavers who taught me but I realize that I will always be connected with my Māori history even though I choose to create my own style."

Claire Matena

Pepeha

Tūranga and Ruapehu are the mountains
Ōngarue and Whanganui the rivers
Tainui and Aotea the waka
Leslie Matena and Pare Otimi are my parents
My name is Claire Matena
I'm from Taumarunui

❧ ❧

"I was born into a generation where speaking Māori was not a priority. My grandparents were punished for speaking Māori at school; therefore my parents were brought up with English as their first language. The only time I heard my grandparents speak Māori was when they didn't want us to know what they were talking about.

Being Māori and working in Early Childhood (Kindergarten, where Māori is the basis language) had its advantages to develop my language. In the early 80's there weren't many places to go so I enrolled in a night class at the local High school. From there I went on to Massey University to do extra mural classes.

Over the following years my main focus was to improve my reo Māori as much as possible as I had my heart set on going to work at Mana Tamariki Kōhanga Reo (Māori language nest). In 1994 I joined the Māori School Te Ataarangi and with that my discovery of the language really began.

Three years later I finally got into Mana Tamariki Kōhanga Reo. This was a total immersion environment where Māori was spoken day in and day out. The focus was on the children and enhancing their development in all aspects of Māori. I was in "Māori Language Heaven". I wouldn't be where I am today if it wasn't for Mana Tamariki and Te Ataarangi who have been the main players on my journey."

My language, the awakening of my being
My language, my growing desire within
My fulfilment in mind, body and soul

Claire Matena

Pepeha

Ko Tūranga, ko Ruapehu ngā maunga
Ko Ōngarue, ko Whanganui ngā awa
Ko Tainui, ko Aotea ngā waka
Ko Leslie Matena rāua ko Pare Otimi ōku mātua
Ko Claire Matena tōku ingoa
Nō Taumarunui ahau

৵৹

"I whānau ake au i te reanga rawa kore ki te whakamana i te reo Māori. I maukinotia ōku tūpuna nā tā rātou kaha ki te kōrero Māori ki roto i te kura. Kātahi rā ōku mātua ka tipu ake i te reo Tauiwi kē, te reo Ingārehi hei reo tuatahi. Kotahi noa iho te wā i kōrerotia ai te reo Māori e ōku tūpuna, arā noa atu te wā e kore e hiahiatia ana ki a mātou te rongo atu ki tā rātou i kōrero ai.

Hei Māori, me taku mahi ki roto kōhanga kōpuapua kaha ki te reo, he mea pai kia whakapakari ake ai taku reo. Nō te tīmatanga o ngā tau waru tekau, torutoru noa iho ngā wāhi kia haere ai, kātahi ka uru akonga ai au ki tētehi kāreti i te pō, he kura tuarua. Mai i konei ka eke atu ki roto Te Kunenga ki Pūrehuroa (Massey University) ako tene ai.

Rere noa ngā tau, kātahi ka whai tūturu i taku reo Māori, ko tōku kōingo kia eke ki roto i te Kōhanga Reo o Mana Tamariki mahi ai. Nō taku tūhonotanga ki Te Ataarangi i te tau 1994, kātahi anō au ka kitea tūturu te reo, ako pakari ai.

E toru tau ki muri nei, kātahi ka eke maioha ki roto i te Kōhanga Reo o Te Mana Tamariki. He wāhi rūmaki hōhonu i te reo ia rā, ia rā, ko te pūtake kia kauhau ai te tamaiti ki ngā āhuatanga katoa o ngāi tāua te Māori. Kei runga noa atu ahau ki te ihinga o ngā rangi. Ki te kore au te uru atu ki roto o Te Mana Tamariki me Te Ataarangi ka kore rā anō hoki tōku waka e eke ana ki uta. He mea tino maitai te tokorua nei ki a au, ki taku ekenga tapuwae ki tua."

Tōku reo tōku ohooho
Tōku reo tōku māpihi maurea
Tōku whakakai mārihi

Piripi Kīngi Waretini

Pepeha

Ko Tainui te waka

Ko Ōwhawhe, ko Mōtakiora, ko Kariori ngā maunga

Ko Waitomo, ko Te Manga ō Kewa ngā awa

Ko Whaingaroa te moana

Ko Tokikapu, Ko Te Tōkanganui a Noho

Ko Poihākena ngā marae

Ko Ngāti Uekaha, ko Ngāti Rora, Ko Tainui Āwhiro au

Ko Waikato/Maniapoto te iwi

Ko Piripi Kīngi Waretini tōku ingoa

"Kō te tau ono tekau te wā, ko Whaingaroa ki te hau-a-uru o Te Ika a Māui, he wāhi whai raumati hākinakina retireti ngaru, harikoakoa hīhiri takutai moana, ko Poihākena hoki te marae. Ki tua whenua, te marae o Te Tōkanganui-a-Noho ki Te Kuiti, anō hoki te rite, he huihuinga, he tangihanga, he kai, he moe, he waiata, he katakata, he tākaro, he karakia, he whakatau pūkenga wai ki mua aroaro kaumātua kuia, koroua, anō he ōranga Māori tūturu.

Eke tapuwae ki te ao Tauiwi kē, te rama hinātore tāone nui a te Pākehā, taukiri te ohorere ki rō 'mīhini tauiwi' whakamaungia hīnaki ai! Ka tau ihu pae rāwhiti ki mua aroaro pae hau-a-uru, tua whenua ki te tāone nui, aue te marangai ngeru kurī, he pakanga puhapuha whawhai tikanga. He kaitoi whakaari, he kaitoi a Rēhua, he kaipāho reo irirangi a parakuihi, he kaiwhakairo, he toa whaimana ōranga tangata, he kaiwhakarere tere nui ao, he kaiwhakamāori, he kaiwhakatangi waiata, he kaikōrero, he kaiwhakaari, he kaitito pātere oriori, he kaiwaiata, he kaiako, he kaituhi, he Pāpā, he koroua, he tāne ki taku wahine Māori tūturu. He rau tau te huringa i raro *"parahako"* ao Tauiwi kē, engari, pūmau tonu taku manawa Māori hei Māori, *"hoki whakamuri, eke whakamua"*, he ekenga tapuwae Māori tūturu me āna rawa katoa.

He matakupenga hapori "whakahīhī kē te urutomo paepae hāmuti Tauiwi", ki tua, ko te "ao tawhito, ao hou" a ngāi tāua te Māori, he mea whakamana whakapapa ira tangata, ki a Ranginui, ki a Papa-tua-nuku.

Ki tōku ao, he taonga whakahirahira taku whānau, taku wahine, ko āku tamariki mokopuna tuku iho, tuku iho, ko te hapū me te iwi e te katoa. Ngākau nui ake au ki te mahi toi, ki te mahi tuhituhi, ki te mahi waiata, a Māori, a Pākehā. Heio anō, ki tā te kii a tētehi o ōku hoa, *"Ki roto tonu i au ngā hāemata awa e rua, engari ko te mea mangumangu taepō te mea hōhonu rawa atu"*.

Ia rā, he mamae tonu te piringa Māori, Pākehā ahakoa he tangata whenua. Mai rā anō taua whakaritenga. He toa manawanui tonu ngai tāua nō konei, ake, ake; he toto rangatira hoki te toto i heke mai.

"Ko te kākano i ruia mai i Rangiātea, e kore e ngaro".
Tēnā koutou katoa. Ki te whai ao, ki te ao mārama, *"Tihei mauri ora"!*

Piripi Kīngi Waretini

Pepeha

My canoe is Tainui

My mountains, Ōwhawhe, Mōtakiora and Karioi

My rivers are Waitomo and Te Manga ō Kewa

Whaingaroa my ocean waterway

My marae are Tokikapu, Te Tōkanga nui a Noho and

Poihākena

I am Ngāti Ūekaha, Ngāti Rora and Tainui Āwhiro

My people are Waikato, Maniapoto

My name is Piripi Kīngi Waretini

"Middle North Island West Coast, Whaingaroa mid 60's; fun, sun, surf and our marae Poihākena. Te Tōkanganui-a-Noho marae, Te Kuiti, central hinterland, same again; hui (tribal gatherings), tangihanga (funerals), eating, sleeping, singing, laughing, playing and praying, absorbing our elders, kaumātua and kuia, being Māori. Places in time, exquisite, unique, a cultural crock-pot.

Enter urban lights and the world of Pākehā, ouch! East meets west, town meets country, a cultural explosion. Actor, artist, breakfast DJ, carver, freedom fighter, globetrotter, linguist, musician, orator, performer, poet, singer, teacher, writer, father, grandfather, husband. Years living the "system" yet living always in kaupapa Māori, "back to the future", a personal cultural renaissance and pilgrimage.

Systemic Kiwi ideology of "West is best" imposes a technical rationale identifying relationships to status, being Māori is an "old and new world" participating consciousness identifying relationships to each other and our environment, *Te ira tangata,te rangi me te whenua.*

My life is whānau (*family*), my wahine (*wife*), tamariki (*children*) and mokopuna (*grandchildren*), hapū (*sub-tribe*) and iwi (*tribe*). I love art, literature, music both Māori and Pākehā. Having said that, to quote a friend; "Two rivers within me flow, but it is the darkest that runs deepest".

Māori, Pākehā relations continue to cost us daily as an indigenous minority in our own country. That is our reality from "ever since" as Māori. We are a warrior people, we belong here, we're here to stay and we descend from humble yet noble beginnings.

"Ko te kākano i ruia mai i Rangiātea, e kore e ngaro" '
'*The seed sewn at Rangiātea, will never be lost"*.
Greetings. Onward, into the world of light, "*Tihei mauri ora*", let there be life!"

Māori-Medizin

Rongoa Māori

Māori Medicine

He manga wai koia kia kore e whitikia

It is a big river indeed that cannot be crossed

Ein natürlicher Arzneischrank

„Gegen alles ist ein Kraut gewachsen", so lautet die Aussage, die die Benediktinerin Hildegard von Bingen einmal getroffen hat. Wer sich bereits mit der Kräutermedizin beschäftigt hat, der weiß, dass in diesen Worten eine gewisse Wahrheit liegt.

Wie die meisten indigenen Völker der Erde haben sich auch die Māori vor langem die Heilkräfte der sie umgebenden Pflanzenwelt zunutze gemacht. Der Regenwald, der ein immenses Potential für Medizin bot, war Hexenküche und Reservoir zugleich. Durch simples Ausprobieren und die daraus gewonnene Erfahrung haben sich die Māori ein unermessliches Wissen über die einheimische Flora und Fauna angeeignet. Die Arzneimittel, die aus einheimischen Pflanzen und Bäumen Neuseelands hergestellt werden, nennt man *Rongoa Māori* und noch heute werden von den Māori bis zu 200 verschiedene Pflanzen für medizinische und rituelle Zwecke verwendet.

Die Māori glaubten, dass das Auftreten von Krankheiten einer übernatürlichen Heimsuchung zuzuschreiben war. Krankheiten wurden daher ganzheitlich behandelt, indem sowohl der Geist als auch der Körper, die Lebenskraft und die Seele angesprochen wurden.

Mit dem Wissen um die Kunst des Heilens ausgestattet bereitete der Geistheiler (*tohunga*) aus Pflanzen, Beeren, Blättern, Rinden und Wurzeln eine Vielzahl an Stärkungsmitteln und Rezepturen zu. Darüber hinaus verwendete er Beschwörungsformeln und Gebet, machte sich die Wasser-Therapie, die Dampf- und Wärmeanwendungen einschloss, sowie die Anwendung von Massagen zunutze.

Durch sein Wissen hatte der Tohunga die Macht über das Heilige (*tapu*) inne, weshalb die Weisheit um die Kunst des Heilens nur an eine ausgewählte Anzahl von Stammesmitgliedern weitergegeben wurde.

Die Ernte und das Sammeln der Pflanzen wurden vom Kreislauf der Natur beeinflusst, weshalb einige der Gewächse nur zu bestimmten Zeiten im Jahr geerntet werden konnten. Doch genauso wichtig wie der richtige Zeitpunkt der Ernte war es, das Sammeln für Rongoa Māori im Rahmen von *Tikanga Māori* (der Māori-Art, Dinge zu tun) durchzuführen. Durch das Beachten von Tikanga wurde gewährleistet, dass die Pflanzen keinen Schaden nahmen und auch beim nächsten Mal noch ausreichend davon zur Verfügung standen.

Wie alle anderen Bereiche der Māori-Kultur, so wurde auch Rongoa Māori von den europäischen Einwanderern klassifiziert. Über viele Jahre hinweg war es den Māori deshalb verboten ihre traditionelle Medizin zu praktizieren, da sie von den Europäern als eine Form der schwarzen Magie betrachtet wurde.

Diese Einstellung hat sich im Laufe der Jahre glücklicherweise verändert und heute wird das Wissen um die Māori-Medizin weithin öffentlich gelehrt. Nicht selten wird der Regenwald während der Rongoa-Kurse zur Lehrstätte erklärt, um dort vor Ort mit den Pflanzen zu arbeiten.

Auch ich habe mich unter fachkundiger Anleitung meiner Māori–Freunde in den Regenwald begeben, um dort einen genaueren Blick auf deren natürliche Apotheke zu werfen. Diese Ausflüge in den Regenwald Neuseelands waren für mich eine begeisternde Erfahrung, durch die meine Wertschätzung für Mutter Natur noch einmal gesteigert wurde. Auf den nachfolgenden Seiten stelle ich Ihnen einige der Pflanzen und Bäume vor, die noch heute von den Māori zur Behandlung gesundheitlicher Probleme verwendet werden.

Ich möchte ausdrücklich darauf hinweisen, dass ich auf den folgenden Seiten KEINE medizinischen Ratschläge oder Empfehlungen zur Nachahmung gebe. Ich schreibe lediglich das nieder, was ich von den Māori in persönlichen Gesprächen über Rongoa Māori erfahren habe.

Harakeke

Durch seine Vielseitigkeit war *Harakeke* für die Māori sehr wertvoll. Die Wurzeln wurden geröstet und als Umschlag für Abszesse und Geschwüre verwendet. Die Blätter der Pflanze wurden gekocht und als Sud zur Blutreinigung getrunken, während der Wurzelsaft zur Desinfektion von Wunden gebraucht wurde.

Mit dem Harz (*pia*) wurden Verbrennungen und Borkenflechte behandelt. Bei Zahnschmerzen wurden ein paar Tropfen des Wurzelharzes oder des gequetschten Blattes in das Loch des betroffenen Zahnes geträufelt. Zerstieß man die Blätter, dienten sie als Verband um gebrochene Knochen zu versorgen, während die Blattfasern dazu verwendet wurden um Wunden zu nähen. Harakeke genoss auch einen hervorragenden Ruf bei der Behandlung von Ruhr, Ekzemen und Verbrühungen.

Kawakawa

Fast jeder Māori beherbergt in seinem Garten den *Kawakawa*, der bis zu sechs Meter hochwachsen kann. Den Namen trägt das Gewächs aufgrund seines bitteren Geschmacks, denn unter anderem bedeutet *kawa* auf Māori „bitter". Wenn man die Blätter zum ersten Mal probiert, verzieht man schon einmal das Gesicht, doch wenn man sich davon nicht abschrecken lässt, dann hat man sich schnell an den Geschmack gewöhnt. Ich selbst habe an Kawakawa große Freude gefunden und jeden Tag eines der Blätter mit heißem Wasser aufgebrüht.

Sammelt man Kawakawa im Regenwald, dann fällt einem zumeist auf, dass die herzförmigen Blätter oftmals von großen Insektenlöchern durchzogen sind. Diese Verzierung tut zwar der Ästhetik einen kleinen Abbruch, doch erfahrene Sammler wissen, dass man die löchrigen Blätter den unversehrten vorziehen sollte. Die kleinen Raupen der Native Looper Moth, die für die Löcher in den Blättern verantwortlich sind, sind nämlich sehr wählerisch und kauen nur auf dem Allerbesten herum.

Die Māori verwenden den Blattsaft des Kawakawa innerlich zur Blutreinigung und Blutverdünnung sowie zur Entgiftung von Leber und Nieren. Eingesetzt wird der Saft auch bei Verdauungsbeschwerden, bei Husten und Bronchitis.

Äußerlich werden die Blätter und die Rinde als Sud zur Behandlung von Wunden, Geschwüren, Hautkrankheiten, Verbrühungen und Verbrennungen verwandt.

Pūhā

Pūhā wächst in fast jedem Garten Neuseelands, wobei die Māori die Pflanze nicht nur zu medizinischen Zwecken verwenden. Bereits vor langer Zeit hat Pūhā die Māori-Küche erobert. Die Blätter und jungen Triebe werden oftmals als Salat gereicht oder dienen in gekochtem Zustand als Beilage zu Fleischgerichten.

Medizinisch gesehen ist Pūhā wohl ein wahres Wundermittel. Die Māori verwenden die Pflanze u. a. zur Blutreinigung, bei Durchfall, Magenbeschwerden und Infektionen. Pūhā soll sich auch zur Stärkung der Leber

Harakeke (Phormium tenax) also known as New Zealand flax   **Harakeke** ist auch als Neuseeland-Flachs bekannt

Kawakawa (Macropiper excelsum); **Blüten**: Gelb, die zu grünen Beeren heranreifen; **Flowers**: Yellow forming into green berries

und als Betäubungsmittel bewährt haben.

Pōhutukawa

Der *Pōhutukawa* ist für mich das schönste Arzneimittel im Reigen von Rongoa Māori. Schon bei meiner ersten Reise durch Aotearoa habe ich diesen Baum wegen seiner leuchtend roten Blüten bewundert. Da der Baum vor allem an den Küsten Neuseelands wächst, bieten die feuerroten Blüten zu dem azurfarbenen Blau des Pazifik einen einzigartigen Kontrast.

Der Pōhutukawa war bei den Māori hochgeschätzt und in der Regel war es der Tohunga, der das Arzneimittel herstellte. Der aufgekochte Extrakt der inneren Rinde, der Ellagsäure enthält, half bei Ruhr und Durchfall. Der Blütennektar wurde zur Linderung bei Halsentzündungen verwendet.

Mānuka

Der *Mānuka* gehört zur Familie des Teebaums und was seine Umgebung anbelangt ist er ein anspruchsloser Zeitgenosse. Aus dem Mānukabaum werden vor allem der berühmte Mānuka-Honig sowie das wertvolle Mānuka-Öl gewonnen.

Die frühen Māori verwendeten die federartigen Blätter des Mānuka zur Desinfektion von Wunden. Ein Aufguss aus der Rinde oder den Blättern diente der Schmerzlinderung und half bei Erkältungen, Blasenentzündungen und anderen Infektionen.

Durch das Kauen von Samen und Teilen der Jungpflanzen wurden Beschwerden im Magen- und Darmbereich behandelt. Das Öl wurde bei Juckreiz, Ekzemen, Entzündungen am Zahnfleisch, Akne und bei allergischen und rheumatischen Erkrankungen eingesetzt.

Natural Medicine Cabinet

As the saying goes, there is an herb for everything. Anyone who has used herbal medicine can confirm that a certain truth can be found in these words.

Like most indigenous people the Māori took advantage of the healing powers of the surrounding vegetation. The rain forest was like a witch's kitchen as it offered a huge selection of ingredients for Māori medicine. By simple trial and error they learned to use the plants to fight health problems and diseases. Over the years Māori have collected an immense storehouse of information about the indigenous flora and fauna.

The term *Rongoa Māori* describes the natural medicine that is made from native plants of New Zealand. Today up to 200 different plants are used by the Māori people for medicinal and ritual purposes.

In former times the Māori believed that disease was attributed to supernatural visitation. Therefore, illnesses were treated holistically by addressing body and mind the life force (*mauri*) and the spirit (*wairua*).

Endowed with the knowledge of Māori medicine, the Māori spiritual healer (*tohunga*) prepared tonics and recipes, used incantations (*karakia*) and prayer, water therapy (*wai tapu*) or massage (*mirimiri*). The ingredients for the natural medicine were taken from plants, berries, leaves, barks and roots. By his knowledge the tohunga was considered to be sacred (*tapu*) and therefore the knowledge about Rongoa Māori was passed on only to a selected number of tribal members.

The cycle of nature dominated the time of harvesting and collection of the plants. Some of the plants were only available at certain times of the year. Just as important as the time of harvesting, was the collection of the plants in the context of *tikanga M*āori, the Māori way of doing things. By following tikanga on one side it was guaranteed that the plants would not be damaged and on the other that there would be enough supplies the next time.

Like all other aspects of the Māori culture, Rongoa Māori was also classified and evaluated by the European immigrants. For many years it was illegal for Māori to practice their traditional medicine as it was seen as a form of black magic.

Fortunately the attitude towards Rongoa Māori has changed over the years and today it is taught within communities and more formally through continuing education courses. Often Rongoa courses are held in the bush, where all the natural medicine can be found in great abundance.

Several times I took a closer look at the "natural pharmacy" of the Māori people when I visited New Zealand's rain forest with my friend June and the Māori chef Charles Royal. These excursions were an inspiring experience for me, which helped me to increase my appreciation and gratefulness for Mother Nature.

On the following pages I will introduce you to some of the best known plants and trees, which are still used for Rongoa Māori.

I want to emphasise that I am NOT giving any medical advice or recommendations on the next pages how to treat diseases or indispositions with a special remedy. I am only presenting information about Rongoa Māori that I have learned in personal conversations with the Māori people.

Harakeke

Due to its versatility *harakeke* was of great use to the Māori people. The roots were roasted and used as cold applications for abscesses and ulcers. The leaves were boiled and used as blood purifier and the root juice was applied to wounds to serve as disinfectant. The gum of the plant, called "*pia*", was very efficient for treating burns and ringworm. If one suffered from toothache a few drops of juice from the root or leaf base were placed into the cavity of the affected tooth. Pounded leaves served as a dressing for broken bones and leaf fibre or strips were ideal for sewing up wounds. Harakeke was also an effective treatment for dysentery, eczema and scalds.

Kawakawa

In almost every garden of the Māori people you can find *kawakawa*, which can grow up to six meters high. The name was given to this plant because of its bitter taste, as in the Māori language one meaning of *kawa* is "bitter". It is not unusual that people who taste the leaves for the first time screw up their face but if you don't get deterred by that, then you quickly get used to the flavour. I myself got delighted by the taste of the leaves which I put in my teacup every day topped with hot water.

If you collect kawakawa in the rain forest, then you

might see that the heart-shaped leaves are often traversed by major insect holes. Although this adornment reduces the aesthetics of the leaves a little bit, experienced collectors know that you should prefer the holey leaves rather than those that are intact, since the native looper moth knows what is best as it is very picky.

Kawakawa thins the blood, cleans the liver and the kidneys from toxins and speeds up the healing process. Drinking the juice helps with digestive complaints, as well as coughing and bronchitis. Externally, the leaves and bark are used as a brew for the treatment of wounds, ulcers, skin diseases and burns.

Pūhā

Pūhā grows in almost every garden of New Zealand and the plant is not only used for medicinal purposes. A long time ago pūhā found its way into the Māori diet. The leaves and young shoots are often served raw as a salad or cooked in a delicious meal to accompany meat dishes.

From the medicinal side pūhā is a true wonder drug. The Māori use the plant as a blood purifier. diarrhoea, stomach ailments, liver problems and infections are also treated using pūhā. Pūhā can stop bleeding, is very effective as a poultice and also as a remedy for toothache. The milky sap from crushed pūhā leaves is used to treat warts.

Pōhutukawa

For me the *pōhutukawa* is the most beautiful medicine in the selection of Rongoa Māori. During my first trip to Aotearoa, I admired this tree because of its fiery red flowers. As the tree grows mainly on the coasts of New Zealand, the bright flowers make a unique contrast to the azure blue colour of the Pacific. The pōhutukawa is highly appreciated by Māori and it was usually the *tohunga* who extracted the medicine. When infused, the inner bark treats dysentery and diarrhoea as the tree contains ellagic acid. The flower nectar is used to relieve sore throats.

Mānuka

The *mānuka* belongs to the family of the tea tree and in terms of its environment he is an unassuming fellow. From the mānuka tree the famous mānuka honey and the valuable mānuka oil is obtained.

Early Māori used the feathery leaves of the mānuka to disinfect wounds. An infusion of the bark or the leaves was used to treat colds and cystitis and other infections. It also served for pain relief.

By chewing seeds and parts of the young plants symptoms in the gastro-intestinal tract were treated. Today the oil is used for itching, eczema, inflammation of the gums, acne and allergic and rheumatic diseases.

Pōhutukawa (Metrosideros excelsa); **Blüten:** Feuerrot, puschelartig; **Flowers:** Piercing, flame coloured pom-pom shaped blooms

Mānuka (Leptospermum scoparium)

Māori-Kunst

Ngā Toi Māori

Māori Art

Kei te kamakama te tikanga

It is a proper thing to be joyful and full of high spirits

Das kulturelle Erbe der Māori hat sich schon immer durch die Kunst ausgedrückt. Da es bei den Māori lange Zeit keine geschriebene Sprache gab, war die Kunst das Mittel um erlangtes Wissen weiterzugeben und das Vermächtnis der Vorfahren und ihre Geschichte zu bewahren. Noch heute werden die überlieferten Symbole in aufwendige Kunstwerke integriert und bereiten so dem Künstler als auch seinen Vorfahren Ehre.

Die künstlerische Aktivität kann sich in Form des Schnitzens, Webens, Malens oder Tätowierens ausdrücken. Es gibt Māori, die sich auf das Spielen alter Musikinstrumente, sogenannter *taonga pūoro*, konzentriert haben, andere sind in Tanzgruppen tätig, komponieren Lieder oder gehen der geschätzten Kunst des Geschichtenerzählens nach.

Tā Moko – Kunst auf Körpern

Gleich bei meinem ersten Besuch in Aotearoa im Jahr 1992 sind mir die aufwendigen Tätowierungen (*tā moko*) aufgefallen, die viele Māori-Männer auf ihren Schultern, Oberarmen, Schenkeln oder im Gesicht trugen. Die Muster sind oft großflächig und scheinen geradezu darauf ausgerichtet zu sein, immer mehr von der Haut des Trägers zu vereinnahmen. Bei Frauen sind die Tätowierungen gewöhnlich dezenter und kleiner, befinden sich auf dem Rücken, den Beinen, den Armen oder den Händen. Vereinzelt trifft man Frauen, deren Lippen tätowiert sind oder die auf dem Kinn wunderschön gestaltete Muster tragen, sogenannte *moko kauae*.

Während ich Informationen über das Tā Moko sammelte hatte ich öfters Gelegenheit, den Künstler Daniel Ormsby vom Stamm der Ngāti Maniapoto bei seiner Arbeit zu beobachten. Als ich das erste Mal in Daniels Haus kam, zeichnete er ein kunstvolles Muster auf den Oberarm seines Kunden. Den ganzen Vormittag war Daniel bereits damit beschäftigt. Die Arbeit des Tätowierens würde weitere Stunden in Anspruch nehmen und mehrere Sitzungen erfordern. Während Daniel seiner Arbeit nachging, erläuterte er mir die Bedeutung des Tā Moko und führte mich so in ein bedeutendes Thema der Māori-Kultur ein.

Eine Kunstform mit Geschichte

Seit Anbeginn ist das Tā Moko bei den Māori eine weitverbreitete Art des Körperschmucks. Bereits die ersten Europäer, die Ende des 18ten Jahrhunderts neuseeländischen Boden betraten und Kontakt mit der indigenen Bevölkerung hatten, bestaunten die vielfältigen Ornamente auf deren Haut. Der Gedanke der Verschönerung spielte bei den Kriegern allerdings nur eine geringe Rolle. Die Tätowierung war in erster Linie eine Art Identifikationskarte, an der die

Stellung, die Abstammung und die bisherigen Errungenschaften des Trägers abzulesen waren. In der Konfrontation mit dem Feind diente die Gesichtstätowierung auch dazu, dem Gegenüber Furcht und Respekt einzuflößen.

Die meisten Menschen bringen den Begriff „tätowieren" automatisch mit Schmerzen in Verbindung. Dieser Gedanke ist natürlich naheliegend, vor allem wenn man einem Tätowierer dabei zusieht, wie er nach und nach das Motiv in die Haut eingraviert. In früherer Zeit war das Tätowieren ein äußerst schmerzhafter Prozess, der mit der heutigen Methode in keiner Weise zu vergleichen ist. Während des Tätowierens wurden verschiedene Meißel (*uhi*) verwendet, die aus Albatrossknochen oder Haizähnen hergestellt wurden. An dem Knochenmeißel wurde ein Griff befestigt, und mit einem leichten Hammer wurde das Muster in die Haut geschnitten. Um die Form sichtbar zu machen, wurde das Werkzeug in verschiedenfarbige Pflanzenpigmente eingetaucht und in die offene Haut eingebracht. Wegen dieser Methode wurde das frühere Tätowieren mit dem „Schnitzen in die Haut" verglichen.

Doch nicht nur das Tätowieren war schmerzhaft, auch der Heilungsprozess war mit Leid verbunden. Von den tapferen Kriegern wurde allerdings erwartet, die damit einhergehenden Qualen souverän und mit stoischer Ruhe zu ertragen. Während der Heilung wurden die Krieger unter das Gesetz des *tapu* (heilig) gestellt. Dadurch war es ihnen nicht erlaubt, Essen, das als profan angesehen wurde, zu berühren, so dass sie von anderen versorgt werden mussten. Die Heilung der Haut war zeitintensiv und die Bildung von Narben war eine natürliche Konsequenz der Tätowiermethode.

Ausführender der Tā Moko-Kunst war ein Fachmann, der sogenannte *tohunga-tā-moko* der in der Gemeinschaft ein hohes Ansehen genoss. Bevor der Tätowierer mit seiner Arbeit begann, studierte er sorgfältig die Knochenstruktur der zu tätowierenden Person, um so das perfekte Design zu entwickeln.

Ein Gefährte fürs Leben

Wenn einem in der westlichen Gesellschaft der Sinn nach einer Tätowierung steht, dann geht man in ein Tattoo-Studio um sich dort aus einem Katalog das gewünschte Motiv auszusuchen - eine Vorgehensweise, die bei den Māori undenkbar ist.

Wenn sich ein Māori mit dem Gedanken an ein Tā Moko trägt, dann ist diese Entscheidung lange gereift und oftmals auf ein einschneidendes Ereignis im Leben zurückzuführen. Der Anlass kann das erfolgreiche Überwinden einer schwierigen Situation sein oder die Entscheidung, sich intensiv dem Erlernen oder Vermitteln der Māori-Sprache zu widmen. Kein Māori der seine Kultur ernst nimmt, wird sich leichtfertig für ein Tā Moko entscheiden, denn er ist sich stets der Verantwortung bewusst, die er damit auf sich nimmt. Daher wird dieser Wunsch auch immer von den Familienangehörigen mitgetragen.

Besonders hohe Anforderungen werden an den potentiellen Empfänger und an den Tätowierenden gestellt wenn es um das Ansinnen geht, das Gesicht mit einer Tätowierung schmücken zu lassen. Die Gesichtstätowierung ist eine besondere Auszeichnung, die nur ausgewählten Māori zuteil wird. Zumeist haben sich diese Personen bei der Bewahrung der Māori-Kultur besonders verdient gemacht. Diese Art der Tätowierung darf deshalb auch nur von jemandem ausgeführt werden, der über die erforderliche Qualifikation, das entsprechende Wissen und die dafür notwendige Autorität verfügt.

Das Design des Tā Moko wird von dem Tätowierer individuell gestaltet. In einem persönlichen Gespräch versucht dieser zunächst herauszufinden, welchem Zweck die Tätowierung dienen soll. Jede Linie, jedes Symbol, jedes noch so kleine Detail des Tā Moko erzählt eine Geschichte, die zusammengefasst das individuelle *whakapapa*, die Genealogie des Trägers, darstellt. Das Tā Moko wird somit ein wesentlicher Teil dieses Menschen, es lebt und stirbt mit ihm.

So fasziniert die Europäischen Einwanderer zunächst von dem Körperschmuck der Māori waren, so entschieden lehnten sie ihn nach einiger Zeit ab. Im Jahr 1907 wurde das Tragen des Tā Moko illegal. Dieses Verbot war ein weiterer Schritt der Herabsetzung der Māori-Gesellschaft. Nach und nach waren die Māori um ihre Ländereien, ihre Bräuche, ihre Sprache, ihre Traditionen, und damit um den Stolz auf ihre Herkunft gebracht worden - mit desaströsen Auswirkungen. Das Volk der Māori litt, war heimatlos in der eigenen Heimat.

Die Rebellion begann im Kleinen. Zu Beginn der 1970er bildeten sich Gangs und Banden aus den Reihen der Māori heraus und erkoren das Tā Moko zum sichtbaren Zeichen ihrer Rebellion gegen das politische System. Zum Symbol für Gangs und Aufständische erklärt, erlitt das Tā Moko eine weitere Abwertung.

Doch mit den Jahren wurden die Rufe nach der eigenen Kultur auch in anderen Māori-Kreisen lauter. Einer Zeit der Unterdrückung folgte eine Zeit der Empörung. Die Māori waren nicht mehr dazu bereit, sich lautlos ihrem Schicksal zu unterwerfen. Sie erinnerten sich daran, ein Volk von mächtigen Kriegern gewesen zu sein, deren Vorfahren sich durch Mut und Entschlossenheit auszeichneten.

Der Reichtum der Māori-Kultur liegt zweifellos in seinen Menschen, denen es in den vergangenen Jahrzehnten wieder gelungen ist, stolz auf ihr Erbe, ihre Traditionen und ihre Abstammung zu sein. Auch das Tā Moko hat wieder seinen rechtmäßigen Platz in der Māori-Gesellschaft gefunden und ist wieder das, was es ursprünglich war: ein Zeichen von Stolz auf die eigene Herkunft.

Māori artist Daniel Ormsby drawing the pattern of a tā moko on the skin of his client

The cultural heritage of the Māori has always been expressed through art. For a long time the Māori people did not have a written language. Art was the medium to share gained knowledge and to preserve the legacy of the ancestors and their history. Even in modern Māori art the traditional symbols are used to elaborate artworks and thereby honouring not only the artist but also his ancestors.

The artistic activity can be expressed in carving (*whakairo rākau*), weaving (*raranga*), painting (*waituhi*) or tattooing (*tā moko*). Others play old Māori musical instruments, so-called *taonga pūoro*, "Singing Treasures", are active in *haka* or *kapa haka* dance groups, are composing songs (*waiata*) or follow the highly regarded art of storytelling.

Tā Moko – A Living Art

Even on my first visit to Aotearoa in 1992, I noticed the elaborate tattoos, which adorned the shoulders, upper arms, legs or even the face of many Māori men. The patterns often covered large areas of the body and seemed to be prepared to claim more and more of the bearer's skin. On women, the tattoos are usually delicate and small, and are located on the back, the arms, the legs or the hands. At times I have met ladies whose lips were tattooed or who wore beautifully designed patterns on the chin, known as *moko kauae*.

While I was gathering information on the traditional Māori design, I often had the opportunity to observe Ngāti Maniapoto artist Daniel Ormsby at his work. When I first came into Daniel's house, he drew an impressive pattern on the upper arm of his client. Daniel was busy with that for most of that morning. The work of actual tattooing would take further several hours and several sessions to complete. While Daniel continued his work, he explained to me the significance of tā moko and by that introduced me to a hugely important aspect of Māori culture.

A Historical Art Form

Since the beginning of Māori culture tā moko has been a widespread type of body art for the indigenous people of New Zealand. The very first Europeans who entered New Zealand at the end of the 18th century marvelled at the various ornaments on the skin of Māori. Although the idea of beautifying Māori warriors with a tā moko was a relatively shallow perception by these early Pākehā. More significantly to Māori, the tā moko was a kind of identification card, showing the position, the descent and the recent achievements of the bearer. In a confrontation with the enemy the facial tattoo served a purpose to seriously intimidate the opponent.

Most people associate the term "tattoo" automatically with pain. This is obvious, especially when you watch the tattoo artist while he is carving the pattern into the skin. In earlier times, tattooing was an extremely painful process that has no real comparison with modern methods. During tattooing, various chisels (*uhi*) were used that were made from albatross bone or shark's teeth. A handle was attached to the bone chisel and with a light hammer the design was cut into the skin. To make the pattern visible, the tool was dipped in different coloured plant pigments and applied in the open skin. Because of this, the previous method of tattooing has been compared with "carving in the skin".

The tattooing was painful but the healing process also caused much suffering. Māori warriors were expected to endure the pain with stoic calm and confidence. During the healing the warriors were placed under the lore of tapu (sacred). Thus they were not allowed to touch food which was deemed to be profane or to feed themselves, so they had to be fed by others in a ritualistic manner according to tikanga (custom). The healing of the skin was time consuming and scar formation was a natural consequence of this tattooing method.

The paramount practitioner of tā moko art was a specialist, the *tohunga-tā-moko*, who was held in high esteem within the community. Before the tattoo artist started with his work, he carefully studied the bone structure of the person in order to develop the perfect pattern.

Companion for Life

In Europe it is common to walk into a tattoo studio, look into a book that is filled with motifs and then choose the design you like, - a practice that is unimaginable amongst traditional thinking Māori people.

When a Māori is considering having a tā moko then the decision is usually made after a long and careful period of deliberation often triggered by a major event in life. The reason may be the successful overcoming of a difficult situation or for example the wish to dedicate their life to the learning and the sharing of the Māori language. Whenever a Māori decides to have a tā moko, this decision is supported by the family members. Every Māori who is deeply involved in his culture carefully considers the consequences and the responsibility of receiving a tā moko.

Particularly high standards are expected of the potential recipient and the tattooist when a decision is made to have a facial tattoo. This kind of tā moko is a special honour that only selected Māori are granted. In most cases these people have contributed hugely in promoting Māori initiatives (*kaupapa Māori*). Consequently, this type of tattoo may only be performed by a person who has the necessary qualifications, the knowledge and the authority.

Carving Weekend

In a personal interview the tattoo artist tries to find out the purpose which is to be fulfilled by the tā moko; then the motif is designed and personalised by the artist. Every line, every symbol, every little detail of the tā moko tells a story that when seen as a whole represents the individual *whakapapa*, the genealogy of the bearer. The tā moko becomes a crucial part of the bearer; it lives and dies with him.

Despite Pākehā immigrants being initially fascinated by tā moko, over time they came to reject and revile this ancient artistic practice. In 1907 it finally became illegal to wear tā moko. This ban was a further step in the oppression of Māori society. Gradually, Māori were deprived of their land, their customs, their traditions, and their language and by that also robbed of their pride of unique identity - with disastrous consequences. The people of the Māori were suffering; they became homeless in their own homeland.

Māori resistance began almost unnoticed. In the 1970s gangs formed within the ranks of the Māori. The tā moko was selected to become the visible symbol of their rebellion against the political system. The tā moko, the former sign of pride and honour, suffered a further demise in status by becoming an emblem for gangs and rebels.

Despite this, over time the call for the renaissance of their own culture became louder in other Māori communities. A period of suppression was followed by a period of revitalisation. Māori were no longer willing to submit to this unjust fate silently.

Māori recalled having been a people of mighty warriors whose ancestors were renowned for courage and determination. The richness of Māori culture is undoubtedly alive amongst Māori people, who, in the past few decades, have succeeded to be proud once again in their heritage, their traditions and their origins.

Tā moko has also regained its rightful place amongst Māori in New Zealand society once again. Today it is becoming what it originally was: reclaiming its rightful status as symbol of pride and nobility.

Some Māori wear their tā moko on the inside and do not need to show it.
Some believe the language does not make them Māori but the spirit inside does.
Today's world is made of many different tongues. One is not greater than the other.
The language that speaks from inside is the best we can listen to.

Tokowhā

The group of carvers who participated in the Carving Weekend
The event started on Thursday night
The work was done by Sunday morning
The erection of the wooden pole on Sunday morning at 2 o'clock

An Adornment for Eternity

The forms are reminiscent of ferns and climbing plants and I begin to see what could be a taniwha emerging.

For two hours, Māori artist Daniel Ormsby equipped with a pen and a red felt marker has been drawing a pattern on the upper arm of his client Lance. Bit by bit a landscape of lines, circles and angles develop, coalescing into one another to become a tā moko, a traditional Māori design.

Anyone who thinks they can just drop by and choose a pretty motif from a catalogue is sadly mistaken. The tā moko is based on an individual's life history, roots and personal memories. The tattoo artist creates a unique work of art from it that can only be read by the wearer. A tā moko is not just a mere picture on the skin, it becomes part of the body, shows the wearer's origins, their whakapapa.

The red and blue lines form a harmonious whole. Daniel produces a large mirror so that Lance can have a look at the draft. He explains the forms and patterns that give references to Lance's origin. "Like it?" Lance turns in front of the mirror, tenses his muscles and nods.

On a small corner table Daniel spreads out his tools. Choosing the right needle takes a little while. Daniel works in various combinations, shapes and a variety of sizes. A multitude of colours are available although Daniel prefers black and greys which produce greater contrast on the darker skin of the majority of his clientele.

Daniel puts on rubber gloves and pours black ink into a thimble sized cup, pulls paper towels from a roll and stacks them loosely together. He deposits a large dab of Vaseline onto a glass plate, then Daniel takes a breath and prepares himself to recite a karakia, an ancient incantation. The karakia is a powerful source of artistic energy and comfort that links himself and his client to their ancestors.

At the age of fifteen Daniel started tattooing. His first client was himself. Using a needle he tattooed a colourful mixture of motifs into his thigh, including skulls and all sorts of other bizarre images.

Soon after, customers came who had confidence in Daniel's talent, more than he had in himself. He used homemade equipment provided by others keen to get work done regardless of the methods. Nobody talked about safety or health during these early stages of discovery.

Then one day a man showed up with a drawing of a moko he wanted. After completion the man asked Daniel to explain the meaning but at that time he couldn't. All of a sudden he realised that it was time to make a change. Driven by ambition and the desire for deeper knowledge Daniel went on to study Māori Visual Arts. Many friends and peers called it a waste of time but Daniel chose to follow his inner voice.

Three years later Daniel returned to his hometown equipped with a diploma and a better understanding of the meaning of tā moko and its elements.

Daniel refers to his work as a mixture of tā moko, traditional tattoo and kirituhi, a contemporary Māori tattoo, which is often a blend of Māori and western motifs. The underlying principle is the kaupapa, the purpose, reason and meaning. The kaupapa acknowledges the whakapapa of the wearer, and connects them to their ancestors. Māori are aware of the significance of tā moko. Generally speaking, for Pākehā it's just an image, a fashion statement, something without a deeper meaning.

Once the needle enters the skin, there is no going back. One cannot simply erase the lines, but not everyone can handle the pain. Some clients abort the session after a few minutes.

Daniel's mother is English, his father Māori. She can trace her genealogy to her great-grandmother while his father's lineage is documented over many generations. Māori keep their family history in their head and hearts and process their heritage in song and dance. Each generation passes it on to the next so it is maintained orally in an accurate way. Daniel sees himself as a bridge between the cultures and considers it an advantage to be raised in two different worlds.

I listen to the buzzing sound of the tattoo gun. More than one hundred times per second the needles plunges into the skin engraving the pattern. Daniel is very concentrated. Millimetre by millimetre he follows the pen lines. Lance's face exudes dignity. He knows that the pattern that is developing on his arm will be his friend and companion - forever.

Working with Harakeke

Rotorua artist Leilani Rickard prepares a cord from harakeke

Die Künstlerin Leilani Rickard zeigt, wie man aus Harakeke eine Schnur fertigt

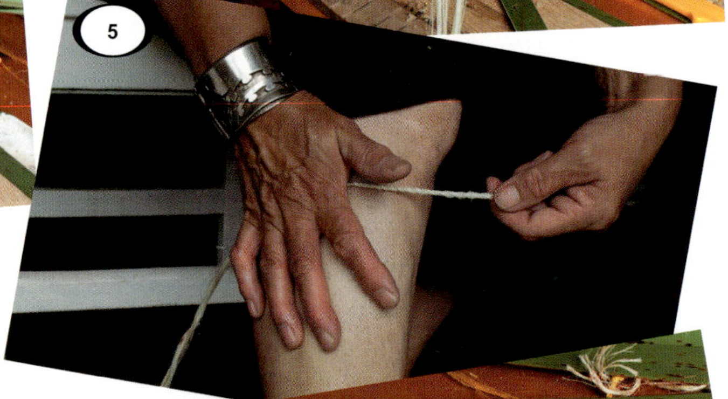

Photo 1:
Stripping the harakeke
Der Harakeke wird in Streifen geteilt

Photo 2:
The pattern is marked on the marking board with the Stanley knife
Das Muster wird auf dem Markierbrett mit einem Teppichmesser gekennzeichnet

Photo 3:
Exposing the fibre with a shell
Die Faser wird unter Verwendung einer Muschelschale freigelegt

Photo 4:
Carefully separating the fibre into threads
Die Faser wird sorgfältig in Fäden geteilt

Photo 5:
Rolling it down the leg unil it interlocks and makes a cord
Die Faser wird am Bein entlang gerollt bis sie sich zu einem Faden verbindet

Photo 6:
The fibre that has been made into a cord
Die Faser, die zu einer Schnur verarbeitet wurde

Pounamu

Geschätzte Kostbarkeiten

Jedes Land dieser Erde verfügt über seine eigenen natürlichen und wertvollen Ressourcen, die von den Einheimischen zu verschiedenen Zwecken genutzt werden.

Eine dieser Kostbarkeiten, die ausschließlich in Neuseeland Aotearoa beheimatet ist, wird von den Māori *pounamu* genannt und bezeichnet die harte Nephrit-Jade. Dieser unscheinbare Stein, der in Flüssen zu finden ist, wurde von den Māori früher zu Werkzeugen, Waffen und Schmuckstücken verarbeitet.

Heute wird Pounamu in großem Maße zur Schmuckherstellung verwendet und fast jeder der Neuseeland schon einmal besucht hat, hat die hübschen Anhänger bewundert, die daraus gefertigt werden.

Für die Māori ist Pounamu äußerst kostbar, weshalb er als Schatz (*taonga*) betrachtet wird. Man glaubt, dass der Stein Macht und Ansehen in sich trägt, weshalb Schmuckstücke aus Pounamu hochgeschätzte Erbstücke sind.

Traditionelle Māori-Designs verfügen über eine starke geistige und symbolische Bedeutung und je mehr man über die einzelnen Zeichen weiß, umso mehr gewinnen sie an Wert. Die Symbole stehen in Zusammenhang mit Mythen und der traditionellen Lebensweise der Māori und werden außerdem mit gewissen menschlichen Eigenschaften in Verbindung gebracht. Schmuckstücke aus Pounamu sollten daher mit Respekt getragen werden. Verschenkt oder empfängt man sie, dann sollte dies mit Liebe und Zuneigung geschehen.

Pounamu

Carved Treasures

Every country in the world has its own valuable natural resources that are used by the locals for various purposes.

One of these treasures, which is solely based in Aotearoa New Zealand is called *pounamu* by Māori and refers to hard nephrite jade. The stone that is found in rivers was fashioned by Māori to become tools, weapons and jewellery.

Today pounamu is largely used for jewellery making and almost everyone who has visited New Zealand has admired the beautiful pendants which are made from it.

For Māori pounamu is extremely precious, they consider it to be a treasure (*taonga*). It is believed that the stone carries power and prestige (*mana*). Therefore, pieces of jewellery made from pounamu are often kept as valued family heirlooms.

Traditional Māori designs have a strong spiritual and symbolic significance and the more one knows about the symbolism of each sign, the more they gain in status. They are associated with myths and traditional Māori lifestyle and are seen in connection with certain human qualities. Jewellery from pounamu should be worn with respect. When passed on or received as a gift love should be the binding force.

Hei Mātau

Angelhaken: Gemäß der Māori-Mythologie fischte Māui die Nordinsel Neuseelands mit einem Angelhaken aus dem Ozean. Der *hei mātau* dient als Symbol für eine sichere Reise über das Wasser, auch die Förderung der persönlichen Stärke und Willenskraft sollen mit diesem Zeichen unterstützt werden.

Fish Hook: According to the Māori mythology Māui fished New Zealand's North Island with a fish hook. The *hei mātau* is used as a symbol for a safe journey across the water; it is said that the sign supports personal strength and willpower.

Koru

Spirale: Der *koru*, der ein sich öffnendes Farnblatt darstellt, symbolisiert den Beginn neuen Lebens oder eines Neuanfangs; er ist ein Zeichen für Frieden, Harmonie und Wachstum.

Spiral: The *koru* describes the new unfurling

fern frond. It symbolises the beginning of new life, renewal, harmony, peace and growth.

Pikuroa

Twist: Der *pikuroa* stellt die vielen Wege des Lebens und der Liebe dar und wird als das ursprüngliche Symbol der Ewigkeit angesehen. Er versinnbildlicht die Macht der Bindung und Freundschaft, der tiefen Loyalität sowie der immerwährenden Liebe.

Twist: The *pikuroa* represents the many paths of life and love and is regarded as the original symbol of eternity. It symbolises the power of fellowship and friendship, deep loyalty and everlasting love.

Manaia

Schutzengel: Das *manaia* ist ein übernatürliches Fabelwesen. Es hat den Kopf eines Vogels, den Körper eines Menschen und den Schwanz eines Fisches und repräsentiert Himmel, Erde und Meer und das Gleichgewicht dazwischen. Das Symbol verfügt über eine starke spirituelle Kraft und ist als der Bewahrer der geistigen Energie und der Wächter gegen das Böse zu sehen. In seiner Funktion als Schutzengel umgibt und schützt es den Träger.

Es wird häufig mit drei Fingern gezeigt, die für die Geburt, das Leben und den Tod stehen. Wird ein vierter Finger dargestellt, so zeigt dieser das Leben im Jenseits an.

Guardian Angel: The *manaia* is an ancient mythical creature. It has the head of a bird, the body of a man and the tail of a fish, representing sky, earth and sea and the balance between. The symbol has a strong spiritual power and can be seen as a holder of spiritual energy and as a guardian against evil. In its role as guardian it envelopes and protects the wearer.

It is often shown with the three fingers, representing birth, life and death. It can also have a forth finger representing the afterlife.

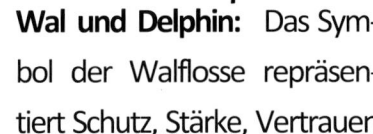

Tohorā & Pāpahu

Wal und Delphin: Das Symbol der Walflosse repräsentiert Schutz, Stärke, Vertrauen und Erfolg. Für die Māori ist der Wal das bedeutendste Tier, denn es versinnbildlicht die Freundschaft und Verbundenheit, die zwischen ihnen und den Meeressäugern besteht und drückt ihren Respekt für das Meer und die Natur aus. Für den Reisenden gilt es als Glücksbringer für eine sichere Überfahrt.

Das Zeichen des Delphins steht für Verspieltheit, Harmonie und Freundschaft und hat überdies eine Schutzfunktion.

Whale and Dolphin: The symbol of the whale tail represents protection, strength, trust and

success. It symbolises the friendship and closeness that exists between marine mammals and Māori people and expresses respect for the sea and nature. For the traveller it is considered as a good luck charm for a safe passage on the sea.

The dolphin is seen as a sign of protection, playfulness, harmony and friendship.

Porowhita

Kreis: Der *porowhita* stellt den Kreislauf des Lebens dar, der keinen Anfang und kein Ende hat und von dem wir alle ein Teil sind.

Circle: The *porowhita* represents the circle of life which has no beginning or end, a cycle of which we are all a part.

Toki

Axt: Das *toki* ist ein Symbol für Stärke, Macht, Entschlossenheit und Kontrolle. Bei den Māori hat das Zeichen daher eine große Bedeutung. In seiner Form gleicht es einer Axtklinge. In früheren Zeiten war die Axt ein wichtiges Werkzeug, das das Überleben des Stammes sicherte. Traditionell wurde es aus Stein gemeißelt und als Erbstück weitergegeben.

Adze: The *toki* is a symbol of strength, power, determination and control. The toki has much meaning to Māori people. Its form shows an axe blade. In earlier times the axe was an important tool that ensured the survival of the tribe. It was traditionally carved in stone and passed down as an heirloom.

Hei-Tiki

Erster Mensch: Die Māori glauben, dass *hei-tiki* der erste Mensch in der Welt der Māori war. Er kam von den Sternen und schuf die erste Frau nach seinem Ebenbild. Die genaue Bedeutung des Zeichens ist allerdings umstritten. Der Tiki wurde schon in alter Zeit als Glücksbringer angesehen, der dem Träger innere Weisheit und klare Gedanken schenken sollte. Man glaubt, dass der Tiki den ungeborenen menschlichen Embryo darstellt. Der geneigte Kopf symbolisiert das Denken, die Hand bedeutet Stärke, der Mund Kommunikation, das Herz die Liebe und die auf die Hüften gelegten Hände sind ein direkter Hinweis auf Fruchtbarkeit. Eine andere Interpretation besagt, dass der Tiki die Zeugungskraft des Mannes symbolisiert.

First Man: The Māori believe *hei-tiki* was the first man in the Māori world; he came from the stars and created the first woman after his image. However, the exact meaning of the tiki symbol is disputed. The tiki has been considered as a good luck charm from ancient times, believed to provide the wearer great inner knowledge and clarity of thought. It is believed that it represents the unborn human embryo. The tilted head represents thinking, the hand is strength, the mouth communication, the heart love and the hands placed on the loins are a direct reference to fertility. Another interpretation is that the tiki represents the virility of man.

Women performing at the Tainui Waka Kapa Haka Festival in Hamilton
Frauen, die anlässlich eines Kapa Haka Festivals in Hamilton auftreten

Waiata Chanted Messages

The singing of songs (*waiata*) is a vital part of Māori culture and plays an important role in everyday life, as well as on special occasions. Waiata have many forms, traditional and modern.

Songs performed in the traditional way can be presented individually or in groups usually without any musical accompaniment or choreography. While all other Māori performance arts, such as *haka* or the use of the *poi* (light balls on a string that are swung on the dance floor) can follow set choreographies, traditional waiata are not subject to these requirements. When performing traditional waiata, singers have the freedom to emphasise words or gestures just as they feel best.

Many waiata, whose lyrics tell of the knowledge and wisdom of the ancestors were composed many centuries earlier. Each tribe has its own repertoire of songs of particular importance for tribe members. Some songs have such beautiful melodies or lyrics that they are adopted by other tribes. These waiata can be seen as a kind of shared treasure and therefore can become a kind of common property. When contemporary waiata are composed, they often tell of important events that affect the tribe or individual.

For an inexperienced or untrained listener traditional Māori waiata may sound tuneless and monotonous, however each of them has their own distinctive musical quality.

A World of Songs

Waiata were generally laments or songs of vilification, in which a message was expressed or in which the composer portrayed heartfelt feelings. Waiata were usually presented in specific public gatherings or on the marae.

Depending on the occasion nowadays waiata are used to entertain, to calm or comfort an audience. In connection with speeches that are held in the marae during the pōwhiri, these songs are often performed at the end of the oration to support and confirm what has been said by the speaker.

The most emphatic poetic power is given to *waiata tangi*, songs sung at funerals (*tangihanga*). This type waiata was composed by both, men and women.

Two types of waiata were composed exclusively for women: *waiata aroha* are songs of love and longing, while *waiata whaiāipo*, so-called "sweetheart waiata" are more flirtatious and witty.

Once, while I was attending a spiritual meeting the speaker sang a waiata. I will never forget the catchy melody of this song entitled "Te Kuititanga".

The first stanza reads:

Te Kuititanga

Descendants of the Kāwau unite
We are Ngāti Maniapoto
Te Tokanganui a noho is our meeting house
We are Ngāti Rora of the King Country
Returning to Te Nehenehenui
To mount Kakepuka Ōtorohanga and Ōtewā
Kaputuhi and Rereāmanu
Where the Māori King Pōtatau was crowned
Kinohaku chiefteness, and Tokikapu[1]
Onto Waipātoto marae at Ōparure
To you, Nanny Rangimarie[2]
And you aunty Digger, what a pair

"It is a modern waiata of love for the tribe, a call to unity and renaissance to revitalise and to recognise those predecessors who have passed on. It is based on the proper name of the town Te Kuiti. Kuiti means the narrowing in, or closing in. Te Kuititanga refers to the physical closing in of the valley that houses the town and simultaneously the strategic unified thinking of the ancestor and Warrior Chief Rewi Maniapoto and his warriors during a time of martial unrest with Pākehā militia. This collective unity provided the impetus for the tribe with which to engage effectively to repel Pākehā militia. Though a modern waiata, the construct and metaphorical symbolism of the waiata is based on traditional lines."

Piripi Waretini

"Te Kuititanga" was composed by Piripi Waretini and Barry Taylor

Te Kuititanga

Ko te kāwau kaki māro kia mau
Ko Ngāti Maniapoto te iwi
Te Tōkanganui-a-noho
Ko Ngāti Rora, Te Rohe Pōtae e
Hoki mai rā ki te Nehenehe nui
Kakepuku, Otorohanga, Otewā
Kaputuhi, Rereāmanu
Te Pōtaetanga o te Kingi e
Ko Kinohaku Te Tapairu e (Tokikapu)
Te Waipātōtō ki Oparure
Aue koe Rangimarie
Te Rangituatahi kōrua e.

[1] Tokikapu Mātua iwi is the composer's marae in Waitomo
[2] These two much loved and respected Ngāti Maniapoto dignitary, mother and daughter Rangimarie Hetet and Diggeress Te Kanawa were world famous traditional Māori weavers and lived at Ōparure and Waipātoto marae during their lifetime.

Haka – A Powerful Presentation

Imagine a horde of muscular warriors who, supported by loud shouting slap their chests and thighs and shake the ground with their stomping feet. And if that is not scary enough, the men stare at their opponent with intense ferocity, the eyes dilating while they dart their tongues in and out like lizards.

Anyone who never witnessed this spectacle before certainly asks the question what the purpose of this dance interlude, called *haka*, is. For the uninitiated haka *is* an indescribable explosion of unbridled culture. Yet it is much more evocative than a mere transliteration can portray. The haka is not just a "war dance". Translated, *haka* simply means "to dance". The haka is a totally expressive dance form in which the whole body is used to portray the entire emotional spectrum: anger, resentment, disdain, sorrow, joy, excitement, all performed with dynamic titan-like fury.

The origin of the *haka* is rooted in timeless yesteryear, among mists of myths, legends and super natural beings. According to Māori mythology Tane-Rore performs the haka. The traditional vibrating of the hands (*wiriwiri*) during the haka is a physical representation of the shimmering heat that personifies Tane-Rore.

Haka is not only reserved for men. Men, women and children can perform the haka separately or together. However, experienced at its zenith, haka is exclusively the domain of seasoned and expert adult men and women.

There are also a variety of haka forms. *Haka peruperu* for example was originally practiced by warriors using weapons. Haka accentuates the strength and courage of men mentally, physically and spiritually to prepare for martial conflicts and was always performed just prior to battle to invoke the ferocity of *Tū-mata-ūenga*, (Tū of the fierce, flashing eyes), God of War to intimidate even the most stoic adversaries.

Haka continues to be deeply entrenched within Māori culture. During pōwhiri haka can be performed to embellish an occasion as with for example, visits of high-ranking dignitaries. More poignantly, haka can be performed at funerals to honour the deceased.

But even in New Zealand's European society the haka plays its role. During state visits, the haka is sometimes included as an integral part of the official welcome ceremony. The haka also enjoys global renown in the sporting arena due to the All Blacks, New Zealand's International Rugby Team. Prior to each international game they perform the famous haka *"ka mate"* to their bewildered opponents. Power, pride and passion "fires and inspires" each athlete while giving their opponents the impression that they are invincible.

Ka mate highlights the indomitability of the Māori spirit. Composed spontaneously in 1810 by Te Rauparaha, the powerful war leader of the Ngāti Toa tribe *ka mate* tells a tale of how he narrowly cheated death. Chased by his enemies Te Rauparaha arrived at the village of the Māori chief Wharerangi who hid him in a food storage pit. As his pursuers came into the village to dispatch him, Wharerangi's wife covered the pit entrance by simply sitting on it. Due to sensitive cultural mores, none of the pursuers suspected the intrepid Māori leader to be hidden in this manner. Eventually, they became despondent and left the village empty-handed. When Te Rauparaha emerged from his hiding place he found an ominous presence standing over him and feared the worst. To his good fortune his fears were allayed when he found the benign presence turned out to be his host and saviour Wharerangi. In exhilaration Te Rauparaha burst forth with an impromptu performance of his now famous haka. The lyrics of the *ka mate* perfectly capture his feelings of despair while he was in the storage pit, not knowing whether he would live or die followed by joy and jubilation at knowing he survived to see the sun shining once again.

Kapa Haka – A Cultural Extravagance

While many consider the haka as aggressive and rude the *kapa haka* bewitches with its elegant and graceful presentation.

Kapa can be translated as "to form a line" and *haka* as "to dance". In New Zealand Aotearoa the kapa haka is commonly known as "Māori Performing Arts" and for Māori it is an opportunity to express their cultural heritage through song and dance. Kapa Haka festivals are held in New Zealand on a regular basis where groups compete nationally to find the "best of the best". Vocal excellence, hand and foot dexterity, individual and group posture, facial expression and the synchronous choreographic performance of the group are evaluated by judges nationally recognized for their expertise in the performing arts.

Kapa haka is life, vitality and power. Every element of the presentation has a meaning that is associated closely with the sung words. The presentation is diverse and varies; Serene dulcet tones of woman can be harshly interrupted by wild masculine screams and vice versa. The guitar, conch shell (*pūtātara*), the *poi* (light balls on a string), weapons (*mau rākau*) and body percussion provide the components to this compelling performance.

Haka Ka Mate

Slap the hands against the tights!
Puff out the chest!
Bend the knees!
Let the hip follow!
Stamp the feet as hard as you can!
This is death! This is death!
This is life! This is life!
This is the hairy man who brought the sun
and caused it to shine!
A step upward!
Another step upward!
A step upward!
Another step upward!
The sun shines!

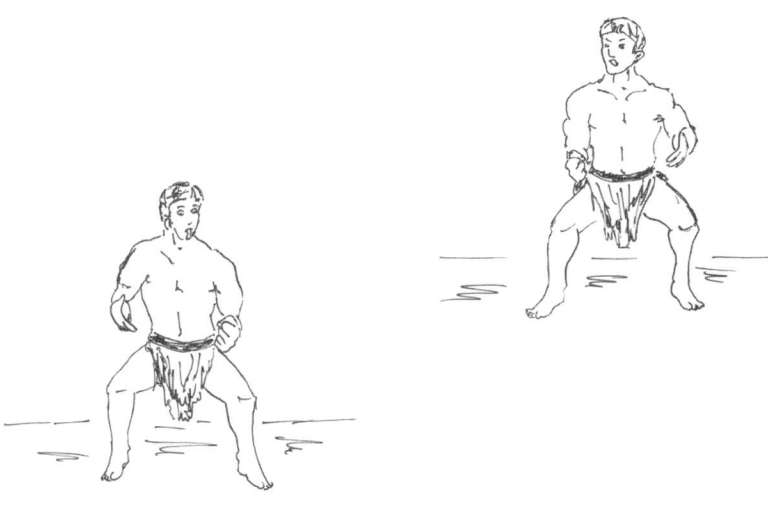

Haka Ka Mate

Ringa pakia!
Uma tiraha!
Turi whatia!
Hope whai ake!
Waewae takahia kia kino!
Ā Ka mate! Ka mate!
Ka ora! Ka ora!
Tēnei te tangata pūhuruhuru
Nāna nei i tiki mai whakawhiti te rā!
Ā, hupane! Ā, kaupane!
Ā, hupane! Ā, kaupane!
Whiti te rā!

Waiata – Gesungene Botschaften

Das Singen von Liedern (*waiata*) ist ein wichtiger Teil der Māori-Kultur und spielt sowohl im täglichen Leben, als auch bei besonderen Anlässen eine große Rolle. Diese Lieder werden in die Kategorien „traditionelle" und „moderne" unterteilt.

Traditionelle Waiata werden entweder von einem einzelnen Künstler oder von einer Gruppe dargeboten. In der Regel werden Waiata ohne jegliche musikalische Begleitung oder Choreographie präsentiert. Während die anderen darbietenden Māori-Künste festgesetzten Choreographien folgen, z. B. beim *Haka* oder bei der Verwendung der *Poi* (leichte Bälle an einer Schnur, die beim Tanzen geschwungen werden), unterliegen Waiata keiner dieser Vorgaben. Beim Vortragen des Waiata hat der Sänger die Freiheit, Worte oder Begriffe durch passende Gesten so zu betonen, wie es ihm beliebt.

Viele Waiata, deren Texte das Wissen und die Weisheit der Vorfahren besingen, wurden bereits vor vielen Jahrhunderten komponiert. Jeder Stamm hat sein eigenes Repertoire an Liedern, das für die Mitglieder von ganz besonderer Bedeutung ist.

Es kann vorkommen, dass Waiata, die eine besonders schöne Melodie haben oder deren Texte die Gefühle eines Stammes in hervorragender Weise ausdrücken, von anderen Stämmen übernommen werden. Diese Waiata kann man als geteilte Kostbarkeiten betrachten, die zu einer Art Gemeingut werden. Wenn in unserer heutigen Zeit Waiata komponiert werden, dann erzählen diese von wichtigen Ereignissen, die den Stamm oder Einzelpersonen betreffen.

Für einen unerfahrenen oder unkundigen Zuhörer mögen die traditionellen Māori-Gesänge unmelodisch und monoton klingen, doch jeder von ihnen verfügt über seine eigene charakteristische musikalische Qualität.

Die Welt der Lieder

Waiata waren in der Regel Wehklagen oder Schmähungen, in denen eine Botschaft übermittelt oder die tiefempfundenen Gefühle des Poeten ausgedrückt wurden. Die Lieder wurden gewöhnlich bei bestimmten öffentlichen Zusammenkünften oder im Marae vorgetragen.

Je nach Anlass dienen Waiata heutzutage dazu, die Zuhörer zu unterhalten, zu beruhigen oder zu trösten. Im Versammlungshaus auf dem Gelände des Marae werden Waiata anlässlich eines Pōwhiri am Ende einer Rede dargebracht, um das Gesagte des Sprechers zu bekräftigen.

Die größte poetische Kraft wurde in die *waiata tangi* gelegt, Lieder die anlässlich Beerdigungen (*tangihanga*) gesungen wurden. Diese Art Waiata wurden sowohl von Männern als auch von Frauen komponiert.

Zwei Arten von Waiata wurden ausschließlich für Frauen komponiert: *waiata aroha* sind Lieder, die von Liebe und Sehnsucht erzählen während *waiata whaiāipo*, sogenannte „sweetheart waiata", eher eine kokette und witzige Note haben.

Haka – Eine lebendige Tradition

Stellen Sie sich eine Horde muskulöser Krieger vor, die sich mit lautem Geschrei an die Brust und auf die Schenkel schlagen und deren stampfende Füße den Boden erschüttern. Als wäre das nicht schon furchteinflößend genug, starren die Männer mit durchdringender Wildheit und weit aufgerissenen Augen auf ihr Gegenüber, wobei sie wie Eidechsen züngeln.

Wer noch niemals Zeuge dieses Schauspiels wurde, der fragt sich sicher, worin der Zweck dieser Tanzeinlage, die sich *haka* nennt, besteht. So erschreckend und einschüchternd die Darbietung des Haka auf einen unerfahrenen Beobachter auch wirken mag, so ist der Haka nicht ausschließlich ein „Kriegstanz". Das Wort *haka* bedeutet übersetzt einfach „tanzen" und ist eine beeindruckende Präsentation, bei der der ganze Körper eingesetzt wird, um Emotionen wie Wut, Ärger, Verachtung, Trauer, Freude und Begeisterung auszudrücken.

Die Wurzeln des Haka sind in die alte Zeit eingebettet und umhüllt von einem Schleier der Mystik, der Legenden und der übernatürlichen Wesen. Gemäß der Māori-Mythologie ist Tane-Rore der Gott des Tanzes, der für seine Mutter Hine Ruamati den Haka tanzte.

Die zitternde Handbewegung (*wiriwiri*), die Bestandteil einer Haka-Darbietung ist, symbolisiert das flirrende Licht, das sich an heißen Sonnentagen bildet und den tanzenden Tane-Rore darstellt.

Der Haka ist aber nicht nur Männern vorbehalten. Männer, Frauen und Kinder können den Haka in Einzelgruppen oder gemeinsam tanzen. Die Geschicklichkeit beim Haka entwickelt sich allerdings erst mit den Jahren, weshalb der Haka die Domäne von erfahrenen Männern und Frauen ist.

Eine Form des Haka, der *haka peruperu*, wurde ursprünglich von den Kriegern unter Benutzung der Waffen vor der Schlacht aufgeführt, um den Gott des Krieges Tūmatauenga zu beschwören. Dieser Tanz veranschaulichte die Stärke und den Mut der Kampfestruppe und half den Kriegern, sich mental auf das anstehende Gefecht vorzubereiten. In der direkten Gegenüberstellung mit dem Feind diente der Haka der Einschüchterung.

Noch heute ist der Haka fest mit der Māori-Kultur verbunden. Im Marae ist die Präsentation des Haka als Teil des Pōwhiri allerdings weitgehend besonderen Anlässen, wie Besuchen von hochrangigen Würdenträgern, vorbehalten. Bei Beerdigungen wird der Haka häufig zu Ehren des Verstorbenen dargeboten. Doch auch in der Gesellschaft der in Neuseeland ansässigen Europäer hat der Haka seit vielen Jahren einen hohen Stellenwert. Bei Staatsbesuchen ist er wesentlicher Bestandteil der offiziellen Begrüßungszeremonie.

Über die Landesgrenzen hinaus bekannt wurde der Haka durch die All Blacks, Neuseelands internationalem Rugby Team, die den berühmten Haka *Ka Mate* vor jedem Spiel aufführen. Mit Stolz und Leidenschaft zelebrieren die All Blacks den Haka und hinterlassen so bei ihren Gegnern den Eindruck, unbesiegbar zu sein.

Der Haka Ka Mate wurde von Te Rauparaha, dem einflussreichen Kriegsführer des Ngāti Toa-Stammes spontan vorgetragen, als er im Jahr 1810 nur knapp dem Tod entronnen war.

Von seinen Feinden gejagt, erreichte er das Dorf des Māori-Führers Wharerangi, der ihn in einer Vorratsgrube, in der Süßkartoffeln gelagert wurden, versteckte. Als Te Rauparahas Verfolger in das Dorf kamen um ihn zu suchen, verdeckte Wharerangis Ehefrau den Einstieg in die Grube, indem sie sich kurzerhand darauf setzte. Keiner der Feinde vermutete den gesuchten Māori-Führer an dieser Stelle, so dass sie nach einiger Zeit das Dorf unverrichteter Dinge wieder verließen. Als Te Rauparaha später aus seinem Versteck heraufstieg, sah er einen Mann am Ausgang der Grube stehen. Er befürchtete das Schlimmste, doch der Mann war Wharerangi, weshalb Te Rauparaha aus Erleichterung den Haka Ka Mate zum Besten gab. Der Wortlaut dieses Haka beschreibt eindrucksvoll die Gefühle des Māori-Führers während er sich in der Grube befand und nicht wusste, ob er leben oder sterben würde.

   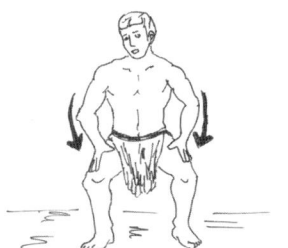

Kapa Haka – Ein kunstvolles Zusammenspiel

Während der Haka vielen aggressiv und eher derb erscheint, betört der *kapa haka* durch seine elegante und würdevolle Ausführung.

Kapa kann mit „eine Reihe bilden" übersetzt werden, *haka* mit „tanzen". Der Kapa Haka fällt in Neuseeland Aotearoa in die Kategorie „Māori Performing Arts" und ist für die Māori eine Möglichkeit, ihr kulturelles Erbe durch Gesang und Tanz auszudrücken. In Neuseeland finden regelmäßig Kapa Haka-Festivals statt, in denen sich Tanzgruppen im direkten Wettbewerb messen. Die Präsentation umfasst Chorgesang, Tanz und Bewegung, wobei die Körperhaltung, die Mimik, eine gute Aussprache und die synchrone Darbietung bewertet werden.

Der Kapa Haka drückt Leben, Kraft und Vitalität aus. Jedes einzelne Element der Darbietung hat eine Bedeutung, die eng mit den gesungenen Worten verknüpft ist. Die Präsentation ist vielseitig und abwechslungsreich und von einem Moment auf den anderen kann der friedliche Gesang der Frauen von dem wilden Geschrei der Männer unterbrochen werden und umgekehrt. Die Gitarre, das Muschelhorn (*pūtātara*), die *poi* (leichte Bälle an einer Schnur), diverse Waffen (*mau rākau*) und die Körperpercussion bilden die Grundlage dieser mitreißenden Darbietung.

Spiritualität & Glaubensansichten

Te Taha Wairua me te Whakapono

Spirituality and Beliefs

Waiho i te taipoto, kaua i te toiroa

Let us keep close together, not wide apart

Auf der Suche nach Weisheit

Bereits die Anreise zu dem Versammlungshaus war abenteuerlich gewesen. Nachdem ich die A30 verlassen hatte, schaukelte ich mit meinem grünen Kleinbus über die hügeligen Weiden. Die Scheibenwischer ächzten schwerfällig unter den heftigen Regenschauern und mehr als einmal befürchtete ich, dass mein Gefährt auf dem mit Schlaglöchern gesäumten Weg von einer Windböe ergriffen, ins Taumeln geraten und mit mir den steilen Abhang hinunterstürzen würde. Da der Boden matschig und das Risiko groß war später im Schlamm stecken zu bleiben, entschloss ich mich dazu, den Bus auf der Anhöhe stehen zu lassen und die letzten zweihundert Meter zu dem kleinen Holzhaus zu Fuß zurückzulegen.

Als ich im Tal ankam, war ich vom Wind zerzaust. Die feuchten Haarsträhnen klebten mir im Gesicht und die Regentropfen hatten sich bereits ihren Weg durch den dünnen Stoff meines Sommerkleides gebahnt. Mir stand der Sinn nach einer Tasse Tee, doch als ich die schwere Holztür aufdrückte, zerschlugen sich meine Hoffnungen. Alle Teilnehmer hatten sich bereits eingefunden und lauschten andächtig den Worten des Redners. Für einen Moment richteten sich acht Augenpaare auf mich und mein Bekannter Tūtahanga, der mir die Teilnahme an dem esoterischen Seminar (wānanga) ermöglicht hatte, wies mir mit einem Fingerzeig einen Platz an dem grob geschnitzten Holztisch zu.

Die Szenerie mutete an wie zu Beginn des vergangenen Jahrhunderts. Der Fußboden bestand aus schwarzem Lehm und wurde wie in alter Zeit mit einem Besen gefegt, der aus trockenen Zweigen gefertigt war. In dem Holzhaus, das lediglich aus einem Raum bestand, gab es weder fließend Wasser noch eine Heizung. Auf der Feuerstelle standen drei schwere Blechtöpfe, die das heiße Wasser für den Tee lieferten. Obwohl in dem offenen Kamin die Flammen loderten, war es kalt. Die Anwesenden hatten sich in dicke Pullover und Jacken gewickelt und ich war froh, dass ich meine Füße in Lederstiefel gesteckt hatte. Am Ende der Tafel stand ein Mann, anmutig und würdevoll. Er sprach Māori und obwohl ich nur einzelne Worte verstand, lauschte ich aufmerksam. Er verfügte über eine hervorragende Rhetorik, seine Rede war lebendig und er verstärkte seine Erzählung, indem er sie durch eine ausdrucksstarke Gestik und Mimik untermauerte. Zu meinem Bedauern wurden auch die weiteren Vorträge ausschließlich in Māori dargeboten und schnell wurde mir klar, dass mir mein Sprach-Defizit nur die Rolle des Beobachters erlauben würde.

Trotzdem war es ein Vorrecht für mich, an dieser Veranstaltung teilnehmen zu dürfen, denn dieses Fleckchen Erde hat für die Māori eine ganz besondere spirituelle Bedeutung. Mitte der

Te Miringa Te Kakara Marae, North Island
Das Marae Te Miringa Te Kakara, das noch heute als Fortbildungsstätte genutzt wird

1850er Jahre hatten der Hohepriester Te Ra Karepe und der spirituelle Heiler Rangawheiiua hier den Bau des sogenannten „Cross House" veranlasst, das ihnen nach der Fertigstellung als Lehrzentrum auf höchstem Niveau diente. Das Gebäude trug den Namen *Te Miringa Te Kakara*, was mit „Ein zärtlicher Wohlgeruch" übersetzt werden kann.

In der Form eines Kreuzes erbaut, war Te Miringa Te Kakara als „Haus der Weisheit und des Lernens" bekannt. Aus allen Herren Ländern strömten zahlreiche Lernwillige hierher um sich u. a. in den Fächern Astronomie, Genealogie und Naturheilkunde unterweisen zu lassen.

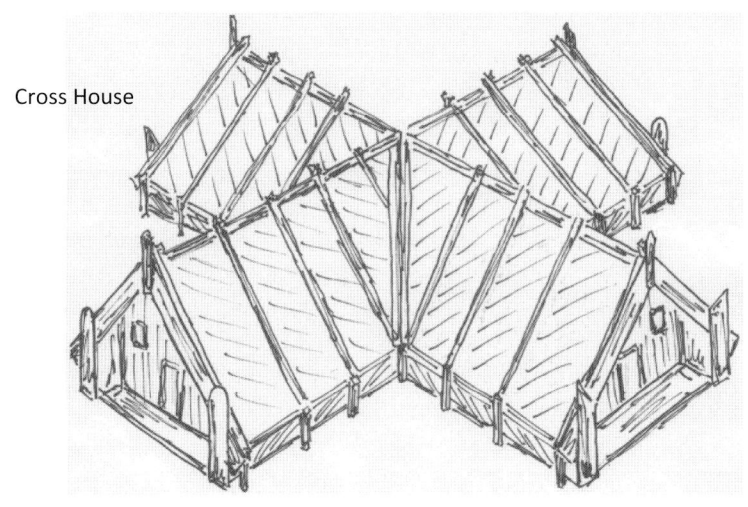

Cross House

Te Miringa Te Kakara um 1900

Bedauerlicherweise war das Cross House im Jahr 1982 durch ein Feuer zerstört worden. Obwohl nur mehr drei Holzpfähle an seine ehemalige Gegenwart erinnern, spürt man noch immer die spirituelle Kraft, die von diesem heiligen Ort ausgeht.

Die Glaubenswelt der Māori

Ein Begriff, der ganz sicher nicht auf die indigene Bevölkerung Neuseelands zutrifft ist „Oberflächlichkeit". Die Māori sind eng mit Mutter Erde, dem Himmel, dem Meer und allem darauf lebenden verbunden. Durch die Gesamtheit ihrer Traditionen, ihrem starken Bezug zu ihren Vorfahren, ihren Glaubensansichten und Legenden sowie ihren mündlichen Überlieferungen weisen sich die Māori als überaus spirituelle Menschen aus.

Tendiert man in der westlichen Kultur zu einer offenkundigen Liebe zu materiellen Dingen, so spielt der Erwerb von Besitztümern und das Streben nach Ruhm und Ehre im Leben der Māori eine auffallend untergeordnete Rolle. Auf ihrer Entdeckungsreise in die Welt der Pākehā haben einige Māori zwar den Ruhm und den Erfolg gekostet, doch zumeist keine wahre Befriedigung darin gefunden. Die Māori wissen, dass sich wahres Glück und Erfüllung im Leben nicht durch materiellen Besitz einstellt sondern in Verbindung mit geistigen Reichtümern steht, weshalb sie dazu neigen, großzügig mit anderen zu teilen.

Im Glaubensbild der Māori gibt es etwa siebzig göttliche Wesen (*atua*), doch nur acht davon sind signifikant:

Tāne Mahuta	Hüter des Waldes
Tangaroa	Gott des Meeres
Tāwhirimātea	Herr der Winde und Elemente
Haumia Tiketike	Gott der Vegetation, Flora und Fauna
Rongomatāne	Gott der kultivierten Pflanzen und des friedlichen Strebens
Tūmatauenga	Gott des Krieges
Whiro	Meister des Bösen

Über all dem steht *Io Matua Kore*, „Io, das elternlose Wesen", das höchste göttliche Wesen, der sich durch die gesamte Schöpfung offenbart. Von ihm wird berichtet, dass er von alters her existiert und keinen Anfang und kein Ende hat. Eine Verehrung, wie sie die Götter und Heiligen innerhalb anderer Religionsgruppen erfahren, wurde Io jedoch niemals zuteil. Er wurde weder durch Bildnisse dargestellt noch wurden ihm Opfergaben dargebracht.

Was die Schöpfungsgeschichte der Māori anbelangt, so erinnert diese sehr an die Genesis. Gemäß der Māori-Lehre brachte Tane alles Leben auf der Erde ins Dasein. Da er sich nach der Gesellschaft einer menschlichen Frau sehnte, formte er in *Hawaiki* (die spirituelle Heimat der Māori) aus Erde die Gestalt einer solchen, bedeckte sie mit seinem Gewand und hauchte ihr den Atem des Lebens ein, wodurch die Grundlage für die Existenz der Menschen gelegt wurde.

Darüber hinaus glauben die Māori an Schutzgeister (*kaitiaki*). Gemäß ihrer Ansicht lassen die verstorbenen Vorfahren einen Schutzgeist zurück, der über die Hinterbliebenen wacht oder heilige Orte behütet. Schutzgeister werden auch als Boten und ein Mittel der Kommunikation zwischen der Geister- und der Menschenwelt angesehen. Kaitiaki können verschiedene Gestalten annehmen, die häufigsten offenbaren sich durch Tiere, Vögel, Insekten und Fische.

Obwohl schon bald nach Eintreffen der Europäischen Siedler viele Māori zum christlichen Glauben konvertierten, bewahrten sie sich einen großen Teil ihrer Glaubensansichten, so dass es zu einer Vermischung der beiden Glaubenslehren kam.

Die Reise nach Hawaiki

Gemäß der Legende ist Hawaiki die spirituelle Heimat der Māori, der Ort, an dem Menschen mit Göttern wandelten und Gemeinschaft mit allen belebten und unbelebten Dingen hatten. Von Hawaiki aus begannen die Māori ihre Reise in ihre neue Heimat Aotearoa.

Noch heute glauben viele Māori daran, dass nach dem Tod die Seelen der Verstorbenen nach Te Reinga (The Leaping Place) zum nördlichsten Punkt der Nordinsel reisen. Die Region ist als *„Muriwhenua"*, *„Land´s End"* bekannt. Von der steinigen Klippenwand, an der ein alter Pōhutukawa wächst, springen die Seelen in die Unterwelt um sich auf die Reise nach Hawaiki zu begeben, wo sie sich schließlich mit ihren Vorfahren vereinen.

Te Reinga (The Leaping Place)
According to Māori mythology at this place the souls of the deceased begin their journey to the ancient homeland of Hawaiki

Ein Blick auf Te Reinga (The Leaping Place) im Norden Neuseelands. Gemäß der Māori-Mythologie beginnen hier die Seelen der Verstorbenen ihre Reise nach Hawaiki

In Search of Wisdom

Just getting to the meeting house had been adventurous. After leaving the A30, I was swaying with my green minibus over the hilly pastures. The wipers creaked under the heavy showers and more than once I was afraid that on this potholes lined road my vehicle would be taken by a wind gust and fall down the steep slope. Since the soil was muddy with a high risk of getting stuck in the sludge later, I decided to leave the bus on top of the hill and to walk down the last two hundred meters to the small wooden house that lay romantically at the foot of the mountain.

When I arrived in the valley I was tousled by the wind. Wet strands of hair stuck in my face and the rain had already made its way through the thin fabric of my summer dress. I was in the mood for a cup of tea but when I pushed open the heavy wooden door my hopes were dashed. All participants had already arrived and listened attentively to the words of the speaker. For a moment eight pairs of eyes looked at me and my friend Tūtahanga, who had enabled me to participate in the esoteric seminar (wānanga), assigned me a place at the rustically carved wooden table.

The setting seemed to be from the beginnings of the last century. The floor was made of black clay and, as in ancient times, it was swept with a broom that was made of dry twigs. In the wooden house which consisted of one room, there was no running water or heating. On the fire place there stood three heavy metal pots which provided the hot water for the tea. Although the flames blazed in the fireplace it was cold. Those present were wrapped in thick sweaters and jackets and I was glad that I had stuck my feet into my leather boots.

At the end of the table stood a man who was graceful and dignified, he spoke in Māori, and, though I understood only a few words, I listened attentively. He had an excellent rhetoric, his speech was vivid and he amplified his story with expressive gestures and facial expressions. Much to my regret all speeches were presented solely in Māori, and soon I realized that my language deficits would only allow me the role of a silent observer instead eager student.

Nevertheless it was a privilege for me to be able to attend this event as this place is of very special spiritual significance for Māori.

In the mid 1850s, the high priest Te Ra Kārepe and the spiritual healer Rangawheiiua had initiated the construction of the so-called "Cross House" that after completion served as an educational centre for the highest order. The building was called Te Miringa Te Kakara, which can be translated as "A tender fragrance".

Built in the shape of a cross Te Miringa Te Kakara was known as the "House of Wisdom and

Learning." From all over the world people willing to learn flocked here to get instructed in fields such as astronomy, genealogy and natural medicine.

Unfortunately, in 1982 the Cross House was destroyed by fire. Although only three wooden poles are reminiscent of its former presence, it still retains the spiritual power that emanates from this very sacred place.

*P*eople with a Spiritual Attitude

A term that is definitely not applicable to the indigenous people of Aotearoa is "superficial". Māori are closely associated with Mother Earth, the sky, the sea and every living thing. Through their traditions, their beliefs and legends, their strong connection to their ancestors, as well as their oral traditions they prove themselves to be extremely spiritual.

While people in the western world are inclined to have an obvious love for material things, in the Māori world the acquisition of possessions and the pursuit of fame and glory plays a remarkably minor role. On their expedition into the Pākehā world Māori have indeed tasted fame and success, but mostly found no real satisfaction in it. Māori are aware that true happiness and fulfilment in life cannot be found in material possessions but demands spiritual riches and so they are inclined to generously share with others.

In the spiritual world of Māori there are about seventy deities (*atua*), but only eight are of special significance:

Tāne Mahuta	God of the forest
Tangaroa	God of the Sea
Tāwhirimātea	Lord of the winds and elements
Haumia Tiketike	God of vegetation and natural flora and fauna
Rongomatāne	God of cultivated plants and peaceful pursuits
Tūmatauenga	God of War
Whiro	Master of Evil

Next page: A sacred site for Ngāti Tūwharetoa Māori, Mount Ruapehu in the Tongariro National Park, North Island

Nächste Seite: Eine heilige Stätte für Māori der Ngāti Tūwharetoa, Mount Ruapehu im Tongariro National Park, Nordinsel

Above all is *Io Matua Kore*, "Io the Parentless Being", the "Supreme Being" that is revealed by the whole creation. Io was said to have existed for all time, he has no beginning and no end. Worship like that which was given to the gods and the saints in other religions was never given to Io. No image was ever made and no sacrifices were offered to him.

The creation story of the Māori reminds us of the Genesis. According to the teaching of Māori it was Tāne who brought all life on earth into existence. Since he longed for the company of a human woman, he formed a female body from the soil in *Hawaiki* (the spiritual homeland of Māori, from which they departed for Aotearoa), covered her with his garment, and breathed life into her. This provided Māori with the spiritual basis for the creation of human beings.

In addition, Māori believe in guardian spirits (*kaitiaki*). The departed ancestors leave a protective spirit behind, who is watching over the bereaved or who protects sacred places. Guardian spirits are also messengers and a means of communication between the spiritual and the human world. The guardian spirits can appear in various forms, commonly revealed by animals, birds, insects and fish.

Soon after the arrival of the European settlers many Māori converted to Christianity however, they still retained their former beliefs. The result was a mixture of two religious belief systems.

The Journey to Hawaiki

According to the legend, Hawaiki is the spiritual homeland of Māori, the place where men walked with Gods and had an intimate communion with all animate and inanimate things. From Hawaiki Māori began their voyage to their new home Aotearoa, but they never forgot the old traditions and beliefs.

Even today, many Māori believe that after death the souls of the deceased travel to Te Reinga (The Leaping Place) at the most northern point of the North Island. The region is known as "*Muriwhenua*", "Land´s End". An old pōhutukawa grows on the rocky cliff face, where the souls jump into the underworld to go on a journey to the ancient homeland of Hawaiki, where they finally unite with their ancestors.

Previous page: Lighthouse at Cape Reinga on the Northern top of the North Island
Vorherige Seite: Leuchtturm am Cape Reinga an der nördlichsten Spitze der Nordinsel

Matarangi Beach, Coromandel, North Island

Glossar
Whakamārama kupu
Glossary

A

Aotearoa
Der Name der Māori für Neuseeland, das Land der langen weißen Wolke
The Māori name for New Zealand, the land of the long white cloud

Arohanui, aroha nui
Mit inniger Zuneigung, viel Liebe; der Ausdruck wird oft am Ende von Briefen benutzt, wenn man mit Freunden kommuniziert
With deep affection, much love; often used in signing off letters to friends

H

Haere rā
Leb wohl
Farewell

Haere mai
Herzlich willkommen, tritt näher
Welcome, come forward

Haka
Darbietung des "Haka", lebhafte Tanzdarbietung mit einzelnen Elementen und rhythmisch gerufenen Worten
The term describes the performance of haka, vigorous dances with actions and rhythmically shouted words

Hākari
Üppiges Mahl, Fest, Bankett, Feier, Unterhaltung
Sumptuous meal, feast, banquet, celebration, entertainment

Hāngi
Speisen, die in einem Erdofen, unter Nutzung von Dampf und der Hitze heißer Steine zubereitet werden
Food cooked in the earth oven with steam and heat from heated stones

Harakeke
Neuseeland-Flachs, eine wichtige einheimische Pflanze Neuseelands, mit langen, aufrecht stehenden Blättern und roten Blüten; gedeiht in den Sumpfgebieten Neuseelands
New Zealand flax, an important native plant with long, upright leaves and red flowers; found in swamps throughout Aotearoa

Hapū
Die Großfamilie mit einem gemeinsamen Vorfahren
The extended family group with a common ancestor

Hawaiki
Die spirituelle Heimat der Māori, von der sie nach Aotearoa gereist sind. Gemäß einiger Überlieferungen war es Io, das höchste Wesen, der die Orte Hawaiki-nui (Großes Hawaiki), Hawaiki-roa (Langes Hawaiki), Hawaiki-pāmamao (Fernes Hawaiki) und Hawaiki-Tapu (Heiliges Hawaiki), schuf, einen Ort, der von Gottheiten (atua) bewohnt wird. Die Māori glauben, dass die Seele (wairua) nach dem Tod in die Heimat der Vorfahren zurückkehrt
Describes the spiritual homeland of Māori, from which they migrated to Aotearoa. According to some traditions it was Io, the Supreme Being, who created Hawaiki-nui (Great Hawaiki), Hawaiki-roa (Long Hawaiki), Hawaiki-pāmamao (Far off Hawaiki) and Hawaiki-

tapu (Sacred Hawaiki), a place inhabited by spiritual deities (atua). It is believed that the spirit (wairua) returns to this ancestral homeland after death

Hongi
Traditionelle Begrüßung der Māori, die Nase zum Gruß aneinander zu drücken
Traditional greeting, to press noses in greeting

Hui
Versammlung, Zusammenkunft, Seminar anlässlich eines bestimmten Anlasses
Gathering, meeting, assembly, seminar for a specific purpose

I

Iwi
Stamm
Tribe

K

Kai
Essen, Mahlzeit
Food, meal

Ka kite anō
Auf Wiedersehen
See you soon

Karanga
Traditioneller Willkommensruf; feierlicher Ruf zu Beginn eines Pōwhiri, um die Besucher auf dem Marae oder an einem gleichwertigen Veranstaltungsort willkommen zu heißen
The traditional call of welcome to visitors onto a marae at the start of a pōwhiri

Karakia
Gebet, rituelle Gesänge, die in Māori unter Verwendung traditioneller Symbole und Strukturen schnell vorgetragen werden
Prayer, ritual chant, intoned incantation - chants recited rapidly using traditional language, symbols and structures

Kaupapa
Zweck, Grund, Bedeutung
Purpose, reason and meaning

Kia ora
Hallo!, Prost!, Alles Gute!, Vielen Dank
Hello!, Be well!, Thank you

Koha
Geschenk, Gabe, Spende, Beitrag
Gift, present, offering, donation, contribution

Koro
Älterer Mann, Großvater, der Begriff um einen älteren Mann anzusprechen
Elderly man, grandfather, term of address for an elderly man

Korowai
Māori-Umhang, der oftmals mit Federn geschmückt ist
Māori cloak often decorated with feathers

Kuia
Ältere Frau, Großmutter, weibliche Älteste
Elderly woman, grandmother, female elder

M

Mana
Status und Ansehen einer Person, Privileg, Autorität, Macht
Status, privilege, authority, power

Manuhiri
Besucher, Gast
Visitor, guest

Māori
Die indigene Bevölkerung Neuseelands. Der Begriff bedeutet übersetzt „normal", „einfach" oder „natürlich"
The indigenous people of Ao-

tearoa. *In the Māori language the word means "normal", "natural" or "ordinary"*

Marae

Die traditionelle Begegnungsstätte der Māori, an der formelle Begrüßungen und Diskussionen stattfinden. Das Wort wird auch oft gebraucht, um den ganzen Gebäudekomplex auf dem Marae zu beschreiben

The traditional meeting place of the Māori where formal greetings and discussions take place. Often also used to include the complex of buildings around the marae property

Marae-ātea

Der Bereich des Vorplatzes auf dem Marae-Gelände auf dem sich die Gastgeber und die Gäste während des Pōwhiri aufhalten; dieser Bereich wird während der Zeremonie heilig; Irdische Plattform himmlischer Wesen, Mensch und Gott

The courtyard area between the hosts and the guest that becomes sacred during the pōwhiri; terrestrial platform of celestial entities, human and deity

Mauri

Lebenskraft, die Seele; der Sitz des Lebens; das Herz, der Sitz der Gefühle

Life force; the soul; seat of life; the heart source, the seat of the emotions

Mihi

Grüßen; eine Begrüßung

To greet; a greeting

Mokopuna

Enkel

Grandchild

N

Noa

Gewöhnlich, uneingeschränkt, frei von tapu

Ordinary, unrestricted, free from tapu

P

Pākehā

Je nach Standpunkt sind damit die Neuseeländer mit ausschließlich britischen Vorfahren, mit überwiegend europäischen Vorfahren oder alle Nicht-Māori gemeint; hellhäutige Menschen; Der Begriff sollte nicht abwertend verstanden werden

Describes all people of Europe-

an origin, who reside in New Zealand; It defines this particular ethnic group as being distinct from those of Asian or African origin, and naturally from those who are Māori; people of fair skin complexion. The term should not be viewed as a derogatory term

Pā

Wohnstätte, befestigtes Dorf

Dwelling place, fortified village

Papa-tua-nuku

Mutter Erde

Mother Earth

Pepeha

Bekannte Verse, in denen die Herkunft (whakapapa) zu einer bestimmten Großfamilie oder einem Stamm beschrieben wird

Well known proverbs that describe whakapapa links to a particular hapū or iwi

Piupiu

Röcke der Māori, die aus Neuseeland-Flachs hergestellt und bei Kapa Haka Veranstaltungen getragen werden

Māori skirts made of harakeke used in kapa haka performance

Pōwhiri
Formelles Willkommensritual der Māori
Welcome ceremony of the Māori

R

Reo
Māori Sprache, Stimme
Māori language, voice

Rongoa Māori
Māori-Medizin
Māori medicine

T

Tā Moko
Traditionelles Māori Design, das früher mit Meißeln in die Haut eingebracht wurde
Traditional Māori tattooing designs on the face or body

Tangata whenua
„Menschen des Landes", bezeichnet die Menschen oder Gastgeber des Marae, die auf dem Land geboren wurden, auf dem bereits ihre Vorfahren gelebt haben
"People of the land", describes the people or hosts of the marae who are born on the land (whenua) where their ancestors have lived

Tangihanga
Die Zeremonie, um die Toten zu beklagen
The ceremony of mourning the dead

Taniwha
Drachenähnliche Lebewesen, die in tiefen Löchern von Seen, in Höhlen oder im Meer leben.
A denizen like dragon that lives in deep pools in rivers, dark caves or in the sea

Tapu
Heilig, verboten, begrenzt, abgesondert; unter dem Schutz der Götter
Sacred, prohibited, restricted, set apart; under protection of deities

Tēnā koe
Guten Tag
Hello

Tohunga
Fachmann auf seinem Gebiet, Priester
Expert, priest

Tūpuna
Vorfahren
Ancestors

W

Waiata
Traditioneller Gesang; allgemeiner Begriff für eine Liedform; Lied, das am Ende einer formellen Ansprache gesungen wird
Traditional chant; Generic term for song forms; Song often performed or sung at conclusion of the formal speech

Waka
Fahrzeug, Beförderungsmittel
Canoe, transport

Whaikōrero
Eine formelle Rede; als Redner zu sprechen
A formal speech; to speak as an orator

Whānau
Familie
Family

Whakapapa
Genealogie, Abstammung
Genealogy

Whare hui
Versammlungshaus auf dem Marae-Gelände
Meeting house on the Marae area

Nachwort

Fast zwanzig Jahre lang verband ich mit Neuseeland ausschließlich wunderschöne Landschaften und langgezogene Strände, eben das, was dem Betrachter gleich auf den ersten Blick ins Auge fällt.

Als ich mit dem Wunsch, ein Buch über die Māori zu schreiben nach Neuseeland auszog, stieß ich nicht überall auf Begeisterung. All das, was den Māori in der Vergangenheit widerfahren ist, hat sie gegenüber Fremden vorsichtig gemacht und daher bedurfte es eines „Türöffners" der für mich in der Gestalt von Tokowhā in mein Leben trat und mir den Zugang in die faszinierende Welt der Māori ermöglichte.

Sieben Monate habe ich in Neuseeland bei den Māori verbracht und was mit einem Alibi begann, wurde zu meinem favorisieren Buchprojekt, in das ich mein ganzes Herz legte. Während meiner Reise durch die Kultur der Māori habe ich mit Aufrichtigkeit und ehrlichem Interesse an den Menschen und ihrer Kultur nach der Wahrheit gegraben. Meine Hoffnungen einen Blick auf eine Kultur zu erhaschen wurden bei weitem übertroffen, da diese Menschen großzügig ihre Türen und ihre Herzen für mich öffneten und mich im Überfluss an ihrem kulturellen Reichtum teilhaben ließen.

All die Erlebnisse, Begegnungen und Gespräche, die ich während meines Aufenthalts mit den Māori haben durfte haben meine Einstellung, meine Wahrnehmung und mein ganzes Leben verändert sowie meine Verbundenheit zu Neuseeland Aotearoa verstärkt.

Viele Jahre hat mich meine vorgefasste Meinung, die auf Vorurteilen und der Darstellung der Medien basierte davon abgehalten Neuseelands verborgenen Schatz, die Māori, zu finden. Ich wünsche mir, dass dieses Buch einen kleinen Anteil daran haben wird, interessierten Menschen Einblick in die einzigartige Kultur der Māori zu geben und ihr Herz vorurteilslos für die vielfältigen Kulturen dieser Welt zu öffnen. Haere rā!

Epilogue

For almost twenty years I associated with New Zealand what any visitor can see at first glance: the beautiful landscape and long, peaceful beaches.

When I set out with the desire to write a book about Māori not all people welcomed me with open arms. All of that which has happened to the Māori in the past has made them wary of strangers. Therefore I required a "door opener" which stepped into my life in the shape of Tokowhā. He opened for me the door to the fascinating world of Māori.

Seven months I've spent with the Māori in New Zealand, and what began with an alibi, became my favoured book project in which I put my whole heart. During my journey through the culture of the Māori, I dug for the truth with sincerity and a genuine interest in the people and their culture. My hopes to catch a glimpse of the culture were far exceeded as these people generously opened their doors and hearts to me and allowed me to partake in the abundance of their cultural riches.

All the experiences, encounters and conversations I had during my stay with the Māori people have changed my attitude, my perception and my personal life and connected me even more with New Zealand Aotearoa.

For many years my preconceived opinion, which was based on prejudice and the presentation by the media, hindered me in finding New Zealand's hidden treasure, the Māori. I sincerely hope that this book will have a small share in giving the people of this world insight into the unique culture of the Māori and to open their hearts impartially to the variety of all the cultures of the earth. Haere rā!

The author in a *hieke*, a Māori cloak
Die Autorin in einem *hieke*, einem typischen Māori-Umhang

He Mihi Aroha

Acknowledgements

*The support I got while I was writing this book was amazing.
I went to Aotearoa with an open heart and a lot of questions not knowing
what to expect. I am still overwhelmed when I think of the wonderful support I received while I
wrote this book. Words are not enough to thank all the people who assisted me.
To Tokowhā all my love, gratitude and honour, without you this book would not have been possible. I am very grateful to my dear friend June, you have been with me all the time. A big hug to
Pipiana, thank you for the lovely time we spent together and for all the wonderful and funny stories you told me. Whenever I make myself a cup of miso soup I think of you and I still laugh about
the dentist story. It will be in the next book, I promise! Thanks also to Daniel who created the wonderful artwork that adorns the book with dignity. Three magnificent motifs that I have on my skin
will always remind me of the wonderful connection that has developed with my friends and extended family from the Māori people. Claire, I will never forget the photo shooting we did together. It was an honour for me to wear your lovely cloak. A big thank you to Leilani and to Charles, to
Debbie and Greg, Tūtahanga, James Tapiata, James Webster, Corey and Hirere, Lisa Ormsby,
James Webster, Moana from the Waikato Museum, to Rebecca and to all the other people who
told me their stories to get an insight into a wonderful and inspiring culture. Thank you to my German editors Helga, Herwig, Karin and Heidi, to Luke who was so kind to have a closer look at my
English grammar and to Wolfram who devotedly prepared the manuscript for print. Special thanks
to my English and Māori Chief Editor Piripi and his lovely wife Angela. You worked until late at
night to keep the deadlines.*

Love you all!

Photo credits

Daniel Ormsby:	4,123
June James:	11
Pipiana Hetet:	13,80
Tokowhā	142
Gülistan Güler:	145,149
Ūekaha Tāne Tinorau:	90
Claudia Edelmann:	all other photographs

All photos taken at places in connection with Māori culture are used with friendly permission of the Māori people.

Von Claudia Edelmann ist ebenfalls erschienen:

Books previously published by Claudia Edelmann:

Tierisch verrückt
Vergnügliches und Kurioses von liebenswerten Vierbeinern
Wolfram Kühnert Verlag
ISBN: 978-3-9813220-0-2
Sorry, this book is only available in German

Der fliegende Delphin
Geschichten & Anekdoten aus dem alten Konstanz
Wartberg Verlag
ISBN: 978-3-8313-1911-4
Sorry, this book is only available in German

Next page: Evening mood at Coromandel, North Island
Nächste Seite: Abendstimmung in Coromandel, Nordinsel